Perennials for Sun

Frances Tenenbaum, Series Editor

HOUGHTON MIFFLIN COMPANY

Boston • New York   1999

Perennials for Sun

Easy Plants for More Beautiful Gardens

Produced by Storey Communications, Inc.
Pownal, Vermont

Library of Congress Cataloging-in-Publication Data
Perennials for Sun : easy plants for more beautiful gardens.
       p.   cm. — (Taylor's 50 best)
     Includes Index.
     ISBN 0-395-87330-4
     1. Perennials.   I. Series.
   SB434.P4745 1999   98–38731
   635.9'32 — dc21   CIP

Printed in the United States of America

WCT 10 9 8 7 6 5 4 3 2 1

CONTENTS

INTRODUCTION

Choosing perennials for your garden can be a daunting task, considering there are thousands of choices. To make the selection easier, this guide lists the easiest-to-grow and best-performing perennials for full sun. Each plant is shown in a color photo for easy identification. The photo is accompanied by information on where and how to grow the featured plant, along with horticultural tips and illustrations to assist you in making your perennial-gardening adventure an enjoyable and educational endeavor.

What Is a Perennial for Sun?

Perennials are plants that persist year after year in a garden. They may be evergreen or deciduous, with the visible parts of the plants dying down each winter and new ones returning each spring from underground buds. Those perennials described as liking full sun need a location with no shade at all, or at least eight hours with no shade.

Where to Plant Perennials

Most perennials make a stronger statement when planted in groups than if planted singly. Suggestions for good garden companions are scattered throughout the book as a guide. Be careful about positioning plants together. Don't plant perennials that like dry soil next to ones that like wet soil, and avoid grouping plants with widely differing pH and fertilizer needs.

Soil Preparation

The key to successful gardening is adequate soil preparation. Unless you are blessed with good rich, deep loam—soil that has been farmed, gardened, or worked to increase aeration, water-holding capacity, and organic matter— you will need to improve your garden soil by cultivation to raise its fertility level and increase its organic content. Soil for most perennials should be turned over with a shovel or spade to a depth of 10 to 12 inches. A fertile or rich soil is one in which there is an ample supply of organic matter and essential plant nutrients in a form that is readily available to plants.

Organic matter is vital to plants; it retains water in the soil and makes it available to plants, and it also provides food for bacteria that change nutrients into forms that can be absorbed by plants. Organic matter is decayed plant and animal remains; the best way to increase it is by adding peat moss, well-rotted compost (either purchased or homemade from garden debris or leaves), or well-rotted horse or cow manure. (Poultry manure is usually too "hot" for most plants, i.e. it contains ammonia that may burn the leaves or roots.) Seaweed is another excellent source of organic matter, but it is not readily available to all gardeners.

In soil that has a high sand or gravel content, many plants suffer from a lack of available water. The best way to increase the water-holding capacity of any soil is to increase its organic content. Conversely, wet soils need to be drained in order to increase the amount of oxygen that is available to plants. Soil drainage can be increased by adding organic matter (or very coarse sand, but organic matter is easier and supplies other benefits). For most perennials, water should never stand over their crowns for more than a few minutes after downpours—the exceptions are, of course, plants that naturally grow in wet spots. In very wet or heavy clay soils, where making the soil hospitable to plants is tough, it is usually easier to build raised beds on top of the soil using bricks, fieldstone, pressure-treated lumber (except near edible plants), or naturally rot-resistant wood such as red cedar or locust. Fill in the center with a mix of topsoil and compost.

Most perennials prefer soil that is slightly acidic (pH 6.5 to 6.8). To determine the pH of your soil, locate a soil-testing station in your area through the state Master Gardener's program (home soil-testing kits are usually not very accurate). To adjust the pH, follow the recommendations of the soil-testing lab.

Fertilizing Plants

All plants need nutrients to maintain vigor. Some plants are heavy feeders and prefer frequent fertilizer applications; others are light feeders and only occasionally need supplementary feeding. Most perennials require a balanced fertilizer (the balance is between the three main ingredients—namely nitrogen [N], phosphorus [P], and potassium [K]) as well as trace elements such as iron, boron, copper, zinc, and magnesium. As a general rule, plants grown for their foliage require a high-nitrogen fertilizer, a formula in which the first number is largest, such as 10-5-5. Plants grown for their flowers benefit from a higher phosphorus content (a formula such as 5-10-5). Organic fertilizers generally release nutrients more slowly but last longer than standard synthetic fertilizers. Calcium, another essential mineral, is usually added in the form of limestone. This also raises the pH; in areas where the pH is already high, use agricultural gypsum.

Hardiness Zones

Each plant listed in this guide has a hardiness rating. These numbers represent the cold and heat tolerance of the plants. Refer to the map on page 123 to determine your hardiness zone.

Mulching and Winter Protection

Mulch is a 2- to 4-inch layer of organic matter laid on the soil surface to retain moisture in the soil and to keep down weed growth. Preferred mulch materials include pine needles (white pine is best), shredded bark, shredded leaves, and bark chips. Avoid peat moss, fresh grass clippings, and hay. Mulch is best applied in fall as the plants are going dormant or in spring as plants start to grow.

In cold climates, apply a 6- to 10-inch layer of winter protection around the crowns of plants after the ground is frozen in early winter, and remove it when forsythia blooms in spring. It is especially important after fall planting to prevent unestablished plants from heaving out of the soil during alternating mild and cold spells.

Planting Perennials

Perennials are sold in two ways—as bare-root or container-grown plants. When planting a bare-root plant, dig a hole large enough so the roots can be spread out comfortably. Before planting, work a handful of a balanced fertilizer into the soil. Fill soil in around the roots and firm gently, making sure not to push down on the crown of the plant. Generally the crown of the plant (where the stem meets the roots) should be just below soil level.

When planting pot- or container-grown plants, be sure to tease the roots apart. If this is not done, the roots may girdle each other and choke off their food and water supply. It is also important to set the plant in the soil at the same level as it was in its container.

Watering

Another key to successful gardening is watering. Provide too little water and plants perform poorly; too much and they're even worse. So how much is enough? First, all perennials should be well watered after planting. This settles the soil around the roots to establish good contact between the soil particles and newly developing root hairs. As a rule, during the growing season most perennials require 1 inch of water per week. Therefore, if it doesn't rain that amount, you will need to water them. Use a rain gauge situated in an open location to measure rain and irrigation. One sure way to "drown" perennials by overwatering is to put them on automatic timers that turn on irrigation water regardless of the amount of natural precipitation they receive.

How do you apply irrigation water? Soaker hoses are best for perennials; sprinklers have a tendency to weigh flowers down with water and splash mud on them, and encourage foliage diseases. A timer that turns the water on and off is a convenient way to use soaker hoses, taking care not to over-water during naturally wet periods.

Controlling Pests and Diseases

Diagnosis is the key to pest and disease control. Ask for help from gardeners in the Master Gardener's programs found in most states, or at your local Cooperative Extension Service; or look for a book on garden pests to help identify the problem and suggest preventative measures and possible cures. Use natural control methods wherever possible; avoid broad-spectrum pesticides if possible—they are harmful to the user as well as the environment and they kill good predators along with pests.

YARROW
Achillea

Zones: 3–9

Bloom Time: Summer

Light: Full sun

Height: 18–30 in.

Interest: Brightly colored blooms over a long season

Yarrow is such an easy-to-grow, decorative plant that new varieties are being introduced all the time. It has beautiful, fernlike green or gray-green leaves and masses of flowers that appear in flat clusters of tiny blossoms atop its strong stems. The flowers appear in a wide range of shades, including white, pale and hot pink, lavender, orange, peach, yellow, and red; they keep coming almost all summer.

HOW TO GROW

Grow yarrow in full sun for strong stems and rich flower colors. Aside from that, it's an undemanding plant and will grow well in any soil except a heavy, wet one. High on any list of drought-tolerant plants, yarrow is ideal for the spots your hose can't reach—or for parts of the country where water is scarce.

To propagate, divide plants in fall or early spring as soon as the first shoots appear. Dig up the plants and carefully pull them apart into three- to five-shoot clumps. Replant as quickly as you can at the same depth and water well.

WHERE TO GROW

Scatter groups of yarrow toward the middle to back of a mixed border—they don't care who their neighbors are; they look equally good with other perennials, as well as bulbs, shrubs, and annuals. Don't forget to plant some yarrow for cutting; it makes a wonderful addition to flower arrangements, both fresh and dried.

Top Choices

- *A.* 'Coronation Gold', a lovely 3-foot plant with lacy gray-green foliage, is topped with 5-inch flower heads of bright gold. It holds its color better than any other yarrow.

- *A.* 'Fireland', also 3 feet, is the best of a plethora of recently introduced hybrids; the abundant flowers open crimson and fade to salmon pink, gradually turning soft gold.

- *A.* 'Summer Shades' is a mixture of colors including antique white, pink, lilac, pale yellow, and rosy red; they blend perfectly with each other.

DRYING YARROW

You can enjoy yarrow in dried arrangements all year long if you take care to harvest and dry it properly.

1 Cut the flowers when they are at their brightest, usually a day or two after they open, leaving 4 inches of stem on the plant from which new shoots will appear.

2 Strip some of the leaves from each stem and gather the stems into a bunch. Fasten a rubber band around the base.

3 Hang the bunch upside down in a cool, dark, well-ventilated place. After a week or two, place each bunch in a brown paper bag to prevent it from becoming dusty until ready to use.

4 Allow to dry thoroughly for six to eight weeks before using them in arrangements.

BLUESTAR

Amsonia tabernaemontana var. *salicifolia*

Zones: 3–9

Bloom Time: Late spring

Light: Full to part sun

Height: 24–36 in.

Interest: Clusters of steel blue, star-shaped flowers; bright yellow foliage in autumn

Bluestar, also called willow amsonia, is a tidy plant with a long season of interest. In late spring, clusters of starry, steel blue flowers appear atop 24- to 36-inch stems. Slender seedpods similar to those of milkweed but not as spectacular follow the blossoms. Then, at summer's end, the shiny, dark green, willow-shaped leaves turn vivid yellow—guaranteed to brighten the dreariest fall day. This star performer requires little attention to keep it happy, although a nod of approval now and then won't go amiss.

HOW TO GROW

Bluestar requires soil that doesn't dry out. Before planting, add organic matter (well-rotted leaf compost or peat moss) to the soil. Mulch with 2 to 3 inches of pine needles or shredded bark to retain moisture.

Grown in part shade, the plants will grow new foliage if the flower stems are cut to about half their height after blossoms have faded. Stems bleed a milky sap when cut (see page 105). Plants rarely need dividing, but to increase your supply, divide into 4- to 6-inch clumps in spring before the brittle shoots start to emerge.

WHERE TO GROW

Plant in full sun or part shade (advisable in the South). To fully appreciate the beauty of the flowers, give bluestar a place at the front of a border. It is most attractive when placed in front of plants with bold foliage such as peonies, hostas, or oak-leaf hydrangeas. To enjoy the fall color to its fullest, plant bluestar alongside plants with bronze or copper foliage.

Top Choices

- *A.* 'WFF Selection', a compact (15- to 18-inch) variety, has the largest flowers and the deepest-colored blossoms of any amsonia. The plant was discovered by the author growing among thousands of seedlings of *A. tabernaemontana.*

- *A. hubrechtii* is a species grown for its feathery foliage, which turns a brilliant golden yellow in autumn. Its blue flowers blossom in May and June. The plants grow 30 to 36 inches tall. Zones 5 to 9.

Garden Companions

Bluestar's delicate leaves and flowers go well with many plants, from those with lacy leaves to larger ones with rougher texture.

- BIGLEAF GOLDENRAY
- BRONZE FENNEL
- BRONZELEAF RODGERSIA
- CORALBELLS
- HOSTAS
- OAK-LEAF HYDRANGEA
- PEONIES
- PERENNIAL GERANIUMS

ENCOURAGING
NEW GROWTH

Bluestar's pale blue flowers will add an attractive dash of color to a perennial bed for three to four weeks. To encourage compact fresh growth, cut off the tops of the stems after bloom. Selective pruning encourages this tough plant to flourish for many years.

GOLDEN MARGUERITE

Anthemis tinctoria

Zones: 4–8

Bloom Time: Summer

Light: Full sun

Height: 24–36 in.

Interest: Fine feathery foliage; masses of golden yellow daisies

Golden marguerite is a prodigious bloomer with bright golden yellow flowers that appear all summer. The bushy plants have attractive, fernlike foliage that provides a striking foil for the abundant blossoms. Leaves are bright green and pleasantly pungent, with an aroma similar to that of a close relative, chamomile. Golden marguerite makes an excellent cut flower.

HOW TO GROW

Golden marguerite must be grown in full sun. It needs well-drained soil that is not overly rich in organic matter or fertilizers—otherwise plants will grow too lush and the flower centers will turn black and mushy. It also prefers good air circulation to reduce the possibility of disease. Golden marguerite blooms so profusely it tends to wear itself out. If the plant starts looking tired, cut it back to half its height and remove any blackened foliage. The plants will respond with a new flush of growth and more flowers.

WHERE TO GROW

Golden marguerite looks great near the front of a border. It is especially pleasing next to a path where the foliage may be brushed in passing, releasing the pungent aroma. It is particularly striking sited near plants with bright blue flowers, such as balloon flower or delphinium. It is not suitable for growing in the hot, muggy climate of the Southeast.

Top Choices

- *A.* 'Kelwayi' bears 2-inch-wide yellow flowers on 24-inch-tall stems.

- *A.* 'Moonlight' has pale lemon-colored flowers on 12-inch plants.

DYER'S CHAMOMILE

Golden marguerite is also called yellow chamomile. It received the name because its yellow blossoms closely resemble the white daisies of Roman chamomile.

For hundreds of years the yellow flowers have been used to produce a bright yellow dye used to color cloth. That use gave golden marguerite its other common name, dyer's chamomile.

A SOUTHEASTERN SUBSTITUTE

Though golden marguerite doesn't thrive in the Southeast, a similar effect can be achieved with another plant called simply marguerite, *Chrysanthemum frutescens*. Flowers come in yellow, white, or pink. It flourishes in heat and humidity. Since it won't tolerate frost, treat it as an annual or pot it in fall to bring indoors for winter.

COLUMBINE
Aquilegia

Zones: 3–9

Bloom Time: Late spring to early summer

Light: Full to part sun

Height: 18–36 in.

Interest: Graceful flowers that dance gaily in the slightest breeze

Columbines add a touch of elegance wherever they are grown. Native to North America, Europe, and Asia, they're delectable, free-flowering plants that bloom in early summer in every color of the rainbow, in both single and double forms (the latter considered especially appealing). Flowers of most species have attractive long tails, or spurs, protruding from the back. The delicate foliage is bright green in most varieties, bluish green in some. Columbine varieties cross-pollinate promiscuously, so plants routinely pop up in unexpected places and surprising colors.

HOW TO GROW

Columbine is easy to grow in average garden soil that is well drained. Plants tend to be short-lived, but since they grow readily from seeds it's worth leaving some pods on the plants to ensure continuity. Be aware that the offspring are unlikely to be the same color as the parent, especially if there are other columbines nearby. If you wish to prevent self-sowing, deadhead the blossoms as soon as they fade. Columbine is sometimes attacked by an insect called leaf miner that tunnels inside the leaves. To control this pest, remove and destroy the infested leaves; new leaves will grow to replace those you pluck off.

WHERE TO GROW

Columbines never seem to look out of place. Plant them throughout the garden—in perennial and shrub borders, and in the rose garden to add variety of form and color. They are are great self-hybridizers, so sprinkle seeds around and watch for new treasures to emerge in your garden.

Top Choices

- *A.* 'Blue Butterflies' grows only 6 inches tall; the centers of its violet-blue flowers are edged in white.

- *A.* Dragon Fly series are 18 inches tall and come in a wide range of colors.

- *A.* 'Dwarf Fairyland' is a mix of a variety of colors on 15-inch-tall plants.

- *A.* 'Music' has a number of different, beautiful colors on 18-inch-tall plants.

Garden Companions

Delicate-looking columbines are especially nice planted near large-flowered perennials or those with vertical flower spikes, including:

- ASIATIC LILIES
- DELPHINIUMS
- FALSE INDIGO
- PERENNIAL CORNFLOWER
- PERENNIAL FOXGLOVE
- SIBERIAN IRISES

Colorful columbine flowers dance in the breeze on thin stalks above prettily scalloped leaves.

PERENNIAL DUSTY-MILLER
Artemisia stellerana

Zones: 3–8

Bloom Time: Small, insignificant blooms in summer

Light: Full sun

Height: 12–30 in.

Interest: Densely felted gray foliage

Also known as beach wormwood and old-woman, perennial dusty-miller is very hardy. The entire plant is densely clothed with silvery gray, feltlike hairs that are very soft to the touch. Though dusty-miller belongs to the daisy family, its yellowish flowers are not showy and many gardeners remove them as they bloom. The plants have a spreading habit, growing three to four times as wide as their 1- to 2½-foot height.

HOW TO GROW

Perennial dusty-miller resents wet feet, so grow it in well-drained soil. It will thrive in ordinary soil as well as dry, sandy soil. In ideal conditions, it spreads readily and will smother its weaker neighbors; make sure they're strong enough to hold their own. Dusty-miller's spreading habit makes it easy to produce new stock; just dig up the clumps in early spring, pull them apart into good-sized chunks, and replant them with the underground stems just below the surface of the soil. Though many people remove the flowers, it doesn't harm the plant to leave them on. Some flower arrangers find the spikes useful as fillers in small bouquets.

WHERE TO GROW

This plant can be grown in a rock garden or at the front edge of a border with low-growing perennials, annuals, or dwarf shrubs. It can also be underplanted with miniature bulbs such as crocuses, dwarf irises, and dwarf daffodils, or it can act as a ground cover for a dry, sandy bank. Combine perennial dusty-miller with other dwarf plants to line a path or use in window boxes. It is unsuitable for the Deep South; in hot, humid climates, replace perennial dusty-miller with the annual dusty-miller, *Senecio cineraria*; it behaves like a perennial in mild climates.

Top Choices

- *A.* 'Silver Brocade' has pewter gray foliage on dense, 10- to 12-inch plants.

- *A. absinthium* 'Powis Castle' is a vigorous plant with mounds of finely cut, lacy, gray-green foliage.

- *A. schmidtiana* 'Silver Mound' has very soft gray-green leaves that grow into a lacy mound 10 to 12 inches tall and wide.

Garden Companions

The omnipresent gray foliage of perennial dusty-miller is a lovely accent for a wide range of more colorful plants, including:

- BLUEBEARDS
- BLUE FESCUE
- BUTTERFLY WEED
- CROCUSES
- DWARF COLUMBINES
- DWARF DAFFODILS
- DWARF IRISES

FIGHTING EROSION

Perennial dusty-miller makes an effective ground cover in light, sandy soils where drought conditions frequently prevail. In fact, it gets one of its common names, beach wormwood, from the fact that it is used extensively to fight erosion on the sand dunes of eastern North America.

BUTTERFLY WEED
Asclepias tuberosa

Zones: 3–9

Bloom Time: Summer

Light: Full sun

Height: 12–24 in.

Interest: Blooms in vibrant shades of yellow, orange, and red; makes long-lasting cut flowers; irresistible to butterflies, particularly monarchs

Butterfly weed, a milkweed, is one of eastern North America's most brightly colored wildflowers. In summer, plants are topped with dense clusters of curiously shaped blossoms. New cultivars come in a variety of colors, while the wildflower is almost always orange. When using it for cut flowers, flame the stems to stop the flow of milky sap (see page 105). Butterfly weed's spectacular flowers are followed in early fall by seedpods that burst, releasing their feathered seeds to float like dancing angels on the breeze.

HOW TO GROW

Butterfly weed must be grown in full sun with good drainage. It thrives in light, sandy soils—in fact, it flourishes in the almost pure sand of Martha's Vineyard, one of the many areas where it is native. Propagation is tricky and is best left to a professional. It is not advisable to move plants once they are established (do not transplant them from the wild); the brittle roots snap off easily, causing almost always fatal shock.

WHERE TO GROW

Plant these hot-colored plants with other vibrant bloomers to create a garden sensation. Alternatively, group with plants with white flowers and those with gray foliage, to shine as the stars of the show. Combined with yarrows, coneflowers, sedums, and many ornamental grasses, butterfly weed can turn a dry or sandy slope into a stunning summer flower garden.

Top Choices

- A. 'Gay Butterflies', a choice cultivar, features blossoms in hues ranging from pale to rich golden yellow, bright orange, and shades of red—some of which appear too hot to touch.

- A. 'Hello Yellow' grows to 18 inches tall with sunny yellow flowers.

BUILDING A RAISED BED

Even in heavy, wet soils, you can grow plants that need good drainage—just build a raised bed.

1 Make a permanent, 10- to 12-inch-high edging around the proposed bed using stone, brick, or pressure-treated wood.

CAUTION: Never use railroad ties, as they are messy to handle and the creosote they contain is detrimental to plant roots. When growing edible plants in raised beds, do not use pressure-treated wood, as it may leach toxic metals into the surrounding soil.

2 Fill the center of the bed with loam, organic matter, and sand at a ratio of 2:1:1 or 1:1:1, depending on the quality of the loam. If it's sandy loam, use less sand; if it's a heavy clay loam, use more.

3 It's much easier to mix in soil amendments before planting. Test the pH of your soil mix; if it's too acidic, add limestone and if it's too alkaline, add garden sulfur. Mix in slow-release fertilizer for nutrition over a long period.

4 Spread the mixture evenly and water well to settle the soil before planting.

FRIKART'S ASTER
Aster x *frikartii*

Zones: 5–8

Bloom Time: Summer

Light: Full sun; flowers poorly in shade

Height: 24–36 in.

Interest: Abundant blue daisies over a long period

This Swiss-bred hybrid ranks among the world's great garden plants—many noted horticulturists insist it belongs in every garden. Such praise is understandable. This aster blends well with just about every other flower color and looks as good in a vase as it does in the garden. The plants have graceful 24- to 36-inch stems, and they're little bothered by pests.

HOW TO GROW
Frikart's aster grows well in ordinary garden soil where it can get lots of water in the summer, but where water does not stand in winter. Deadheading encourages more abundant flowering. In the North, protect it over winter with a layer of evergreen branches to shade the soil and keep it at a more uniform temperature. Do not use mulch over the crowns (at any time of the year), as this

can hold dampness that may cause plants to rot. In the Deep South, Frikart's aster is best treated as an annual. Take stem cuttings in summer to propagate.

WHERE TO GROW

Plant Frikart's aster in the front portion of a sunny perennial border, where it blends with most other plants and will provide abundant color for months. It can also look striking in a large rock garden planted in front of a boulder or dark conifer. Its continuous flowering habit makes this an ideal plant for growing in a container on a sunny patio or deck, either on its own or with other long-blooming plants.

Top Choices

- *A.* 'Mönch' bears fragrant 2- to 3-inch lavender-blue daisies from early summer until frost. The blossoms are larger than those of most other asters.

- *A.* 'Wonder of Staffa' bears bright lapis blue flowers that are up to 2½ inches across. The plants grow as tall as 24 inches and bloom from midsummer to frost.

DEADHEADING

To increase flowering in many plants, remove flowers as soon as they have passed their peak. Cut down to the next leaf or branch on the spent flower stem. This prevents the formation of seeds and encourages the plant to produce more flowers. The plants look better, too.

ON THE BEACH

Another attribute that Frikart's aster can boast is its ability to thrive in coastal gardens. The environment along the ocean shore fits the requirements of this plant like a glove. The sandy, well-drained soil keeps excess moisture away from the plant's roots and crown, while the breeze, nearby water, and frequent foggy mornings keep it cool. Frikart's aster thrives in the bright sun of the shore and shrugs off salt spray, making it a nice addition to rock and cottage gardens in beach areas.

BASKET-OF-GOLD

Aurinia saxatile

Zones: 3–10

Bloom Time: Spring

Light: Full sun

Height: 12–24 in.

Interest: A splash of bright yellow, fragrant flowers

For decades this plant was known as *Alyssum saxatile,* but taxonomists, whose sole purpose is to confuse gardeners, decided it belonged in the genus *Aurinia.* (The much-loved annual alyssum, which bears white or purple flowers all summer, bears little resemblance to its golden cousin.) Despite the confusion, basket-of-gold is a great plant and is one of the indispensable heralds of spring—adding the same spark of yellow that forsythia does, on a more modest scale.

HOW TO GROW

Basket-of-gold must be grown in well-drained soil in full sun. It prefers a lean soil—one not too rich in organic matter and low on nutrients. Don't use plant food unless it releases nutrients slowly (as most organic products do) and is higher in potassium and phosphorous but low in nitrogen. Basket-of-gold is easy to grow from seeds, sown in pots or directly in the ground where it is to flower. Cut back the flower spikes after they have finished blooming. If plants start to get loose and straggly, cut them back to half their size immediately after flowering and remove any dead leaves.

WHERE TO GROW

Basket-of-gold looks great in rock gardens, at the edge of a border, or along a path. It is especially fine hanging over the edge of a stone wall or next to steps. It is the perfect companion for a host of spring-flowering bulbs. For a splash of late-winter color, group three plants in a hanging basket. When frost hits in the North, plunge the whole container to the rim in a pile of mulch. Retrieve it in spring as soon as milder days appear. In the Deep South, simply plant the basket, hang it, and wait for the show to start.

Top Choices

- *A.* 'Citrinum' sports pale yellow blooms.

- *A.* 'Golden Queen' is low-growing and has attractive gray-green foliage that accents its pale yellow flowers.

- *A.* 'Sunny Border Apricot' has almost apricot-colored flowers.

GOLDEN CASCADES

Few plants can match the vivid yellow flowers and free-flowing form of basket-of-gold. The plant seems tailor-made to drape over stone walls and pour over boulders or stone steps. Plant basket-of-gold, in well-worked soil a few inches from the edge of a wall. As the plant grows, train it over the edge of the wall and it will develop a most attractive form.

In the rock garden, plant basket-of-gold in a niche among some boulders. Before planting, fill the niche with ordinary soil amended with a bit of organic matter. Roots can't stretch very far in search of water in such a rock basin, so add a layer of mulch after planting to help conserve moisture. The plant will flow over the rocks, providing a stunning spring accent.

AVOIDING "MELT OUT"

Basket-of-gold tends to "melt out" in high heat and humidity. In the Deep South, treat basket-of-gold as an annual, planting it in early fall with pansies.

FALSE INDIGO

Baptisia australis

Zones: 3–9

Bloom Time: Mid-spring to early summer

Light: Full or part sun (tolerates 3–4 hours of light shade each day)

Height: 36–48 in.

Interest: Brilliant blue flowers; attractive gray-green foliage; black seedpods

False indigo has brilliant blue, pealike blossoms on 10- to 12-inch flower spikes that appear around the time peonies bloom. Flowers are followed by attractive seedpods that start out green but gradually turn black and persist until fall. The grayish green foliage has a cool, pleasant, shrublike appearance and remains appealing until frost cuts it down. Its long-lasting foliage makes false indigo a useful background for plants that are later blooming.

HOW TO GROW

This plant is practically indestructible—it will remain vigorous long after the gardener has thrown in the trowel. In fact, once it is well established you almost need a backhoe to move it; with this in mind, plant false indigo in well-drained soil in a spot where you want it to stay. In full sun, false indigo blooms profusely and needs no staking. It will do almost as well in 3 to 4 hours of light shade, with bloom only slightly diminished, though plants may require staking. Start new plants from seeds. If you allow the seeds to ripen and fall, you may find seedlings close to the base of the parent plants; keep your eyes open for telltale gray-green leaves.

WHERE TO GROW

Shrublike false indigo makes its presence known in any mixed border. It can be surprisingly effective as a seasonal hedge or foundation planting, serving the visual function of a shrub in three seasons and disappearing in winter. Try it where ice sliding off a roof prevents you from growing shrubs.

Top Choices

- *B. alba,* white wild indigo, is a 2- to 3-footer with pure white flowers on 12-inch spikes in late spring. It will grow in full sun or part shade. Zones 5 to 9.

- *B. leucantha,* tall white wild indigo, has blue-green leaves and very tall (36- to 60-inch) flower stems decorated with creamy white flowers. Some of the blossoms are occasionally tinged with lavender. Zones 4 to 9.

Garden Companions

The large, shrublike presence of false indigo is an asset to all sorts of perennials. The blooms clash with few, if any, other flowers.

- ASIATIC LILIES
- BLEEDING-HEART
- DAYLILIES
- IRISES
- LILIES
- MONTBRETIA
- PEONIES
- PINCUSHION FLOWERS
- PYRETHRUMS

HARVESTING
SEEDPODS

When false indigo's seedpods ripen and turn black, they are so heavy they weigh down the branches and you can hear the seeds rattling inside.

To harvest, cut ripe spikes down to the top of the foliage and use them in dried flower arrangements. They require no drying-off period after they are cut.

BOLTONIA

Boltonia asteroides

Zones: 4–8

Bloom Time: Late summer to early fall

Light: Full sun in the North; light, midday shade in the South

Height: 36–60 in.

Interest: Masses of white asterlike flowers

Boltonia has willowlike, grayish green foliage on stiffly erect plants that are smothered with white or pink daisies from August to early October. Boltonia is useful as a vertical accent or planted in a large group to provide a strong architectural presence. Backed by sugar maples in their full fall color, this 3- to 5-foot mass of flowers makes a memorable sight. Boltonia is easy to grow. When in full flower, you'll be sure to wonder if Frosty the Snowman has made an unseasonal appearance in your garden.

HOW TO GROW
This extremely low-maintenance plant will grow just about anywhere it receives full sun. It tolerates damp or dry soil, but it prefers rich soil liberally amended with organic matter. Cut the plants down in late fall after

hard frost. Increase the number of plants by dividing the crowns in early spring before new shoots appear. Boltonia is pest- and disease-free.

WHERE TO GROW

For the best effect, grow boltonia in full sun surrounded by low-growing plants that won't block the light from its base—allowing it to bloom all the way down. Plant it with shrubs that offer good fall color and grasses that bloom at that time. Its stately presence in a bed with low-growing annuals provides contrast and will take over the main show when the annuals start to look tired in late summer. Boltonia also makes a superb hedge for summer and dies down in winter.

Top Choices

- *B. asteroides* var. 'Nana', dwarf boltonia, is a dwarf variety that looks just like an aster. Its pinkish violet flowers bloom on plants that grow 14 to 20 inches tall.

- *B.* 'Pink Beauty', pink boltonia, is a tall (5 to 6 feet) pink selection. Because it tends to flop over under the weight of its many flowers, it must be staked or cut back to half its height before flowering.

- *B.* 'Snowbank' is as white as you would expect from its name.

STAKING
TALL PLANTS

To stake tall plants, cut lengths of twiggy brushwood (such as birch) in early spring before leaves appear. Make them 1 foot shorter than the plants requiring staking. When a plant has reached half its normal height, place stakes in the ground all around it. Surround with garden twine if necessary.

COMPLEMENTARY
PLANTING

Plant boltonia with annuals, tender perennials, and bulbs, including summer-flowering bulbs such as montbretia and gladiolus. It is striking against shrubs and trees such as fothergilla, beautyberry, and Japanese maple. Good perennial companions include chrysanthemums, coneflowers, Japanese anemones, and liatris (gay-feather).

CALAMINT
Calamintha nepeta

Zones: 5–9

Bloom Time: Late summer to fall

Light: Full sun

Height: 12–24 in.

Interest: Clouds of tiny, light-blue-and-white flowers surrounded with foliage

Calamint (sometimes called beautiful mint) is a charming Old World species with tiny, sparkling blossoms in late summer and continuing into mid-autumn. It shrugs off light frost and provides a cheerful sight after most plants have given up for the year and there is little color left in the garden. Another delightful feature of this plant is the pungent aroma that fills the air when the foliage is brushed. This treat can be enjoyed throughout the year, even after calamint has succumbed to frost—but be sure to wait until late winter or early spring before cutting it back.

HOW TO GROW
Like all mints, calamint is easy to grow, but unlike true mints (*Mentha* species), it is a tidy, well-behaved plant that is not determined to take over the world. Plant it in

full sun in ordinary soil. Calamint is drought-tolerant, so it fares well in light, sandy soil. The only maintenance required is cutting the wiry stems close to the ground in late winter or early spring before new shoots appear. Calamint is pest-free; it can be divided in early spring to provide new plants. Cuttings root easily.

WHERE TO GROW

Grow calamint in a location you pass frequently to enjoy its fragrance and exquisite little flowers. Next to the kitchen door is ideal. In foundation plantings, calamint adds sparkle. Try it, too, at the front of a border or alongside shrubs such as roses. It's also perfect in a narrow border by itself, underplanted with bulbs. Don't forget to add this plant to an herb or vegetable garden and use it as a cut flower in mixed arrangements. It complements hot and cool colors, so don't worry about where to plant it in relationship to the other flowers in your garden.

Top Choices

- *C. grandiflora,* large-flowered calamint, is the only other species available in garden centers and mail-order catalogs. It has rose-pink flowers in mid-to late summer and fresh green leaves with a more mint-like appearance than its cousins.

- *C. g.*'Variegata' is an interesting selection whose leaves are spattered with irregular cream markings.

PLANTING PARTNERS

Calamint complements and is complemented by many types of plants in almost any color. Plant it on the sunny side of shrubs; it looks especially fine with old-fashioned shrub roses. Calamint is also a good plant to accent with underplanting—planting flowers or bulbs beneath the canopy of a larger plant to add color to the garden without taking up any additional space.

Consider underplanting beautiful mint with spring-, summer-, and fall-blooming bulbs including crocuses, dwarf lilies, gladioli (especially small-flowered varieties), narcissi, and species tulips.

BEE LURE

Not only is calamint a charming garden plant, but it also provides a beneficial service to its garden neighbors. Its tiny white flowers are irresistible to bees, so plant calamint near late-blooming garden plants for more effective pollination.

CARPATHIAN BELLFLOWER

Campanula carpatica

Zones: 3–8

Bloom Time: Mid-summer

Light: Full to part sun

Height: 8 in.

Interest: Masses of brilliant blue, bell-shaped flowers on a low, spreading plant that makes a great ground cover

Carpathian bellflower is one of the most handsome low-growing plants for the front of the border. In midsummer, it produces masses of brilliant blue flowers that are shaped like little bells (*Campanula* means "little bell" in Latin) and nod slightly on 8-inch stems. The plants spread slowly. When in bloom, the foliage can hardly be seen because there are so many flowers. This bellflower is easy to grow and adds bright, reliable color to the summer garden.

HOW TO GROW

Carpathian bellflower grows best in the cooler parts of the country; it does poorly in hot, humid environments. Provide full sun or part shade (especially in warmer regions) and good drainage to keep bellflower content. Deadheading encourages repeat bloom and discourages an overabundance of self-sown seedlings (leave a few seedpods on the plant if you want a few more plants). Slugs are the only enemy; reduce damage from these critters by following the directions at right.

WHERE TO GROW

Carpathian bellflower belongs at the front of every perennial border, where its brilliant splash of blue can be best appreciated. It is also suited for growing in rock gardens and along the tops of rock walls, where it can spill down to make a colorful, cascading show. Carpathian bellflower fares well in containers such as window boxes and patio planters, providing the plants are not kept too wet or allowed to dry out too much.

Top Choices

- C. 'Blue Clips' bears upward-facing blue flowers over most of the summer.

- C. 'China Doll' has pale lavender-blue, almost flat flowers.

- C. *cochleariifolia*, spiral bellflower, is a prostrate-growing species with tiny, sky blue blossoms. Zones 5 to 10.

- C. 'Jingle Bells' bears flowers in subtle shades of lilac, blue, and white.

- C. 'White Clips' and 'Alba' have white flowers.

REMOVING SLUGS

Slugs are ever-present in moist garden spots, but you can reduce their impact. Avoid poison slug baits and sprays that can wash away. Remove slugs instead.

- Pick them off plants at night when they feed. Use rubber gloves so they don't "slime" you.

- Trap them in grapefruit halves (empty) placed upside down throughout the garden. Check and dispose of any containing slugs.

- Sink margarine tubs into the soil with rims at ground level. Fill ¾ full with beer. Empty when "traps" contain several slugs.

OTHER BELLFLOWERS

Peachleaf bellflower, C. *persicifolia*, is one of the most handsome. It grows 30 to 36 inches high and has blue ('Telham Beauty') or white ('Alba') flowers. Zones 3 to 10.

Dalmatian bellflower, C. *portenschlagiana*, is a spreader that carpets the ground with masses of blue flowers in late spring. It is great in rock gardens and makes a choice ground cover for full sun. Zones 4 to 10.

PERENNIAL CORNFLOWER
Centaurea montana

Zones: 3–8

Bloom Time: Summer

Light: Full to part sun

Height: 18–24 in.

Interest: Masses of brilliant blue, frilly flowers over a long season

Also called mountain bluet, perennial cornflower is a European member of the vast daisy family. Its 2- to 3-inch, brilliant deep blue blossoms are touched with red at the center. The uniquely shaped petals are frilled and fringed in a delicate arrangement on a thistlelike flower head. Perennial cornflower provides an ample supply of cut flowers that enrich any flower arrangement. (Annual cornflower is also called bachelor's-button and is one of the most useful flowers in the cutting garden.)

HOW TO GROW

Plant perennial cornflower and stand back. No, it's not that bad! It grows in almost any soil, but it flops over if allowed to dry out too much. It is more aggressive in rich soils, so avoid fertilizing. Deadhead as soon as flowers are spent to keep it blossoming and reduce the number of self-sown seedlings. Like all spreaders, it is easily increased by dividing the clumps or by transplanting the seedlings. Perennial cornflower does best in cool regions and does not like hot, humid climates.

WHERE TO GROW

Perennial cornflower thrives in full sun but is almost as happy in part shade, where it has a tendency to be floppier. Since this plant can be a spreader (especially in northern gardens), locate it with care. Avoid placing perennial cornflower in a border with delicate plants that are easily overcome by aggressive colonizers. Take advantage of cornflower's habit by using it to hold a sunny bank, but be careful not to let the soil dry out before the cornflower is well established. It provides a colorful companion for all but the shortest of shrubs.

Top Choices

- *C. dealbata,* Persian cornflower, has rose or lavender-pink flowers all summer long on 18- to 30-inch plants. 'Rosea' has soft pink flowers.

- *C. macrocephala,* globe centaurea, has yellow flowers on 3- to 4-foot plants (shorter in the Deep South).

CONTROLLING INVASIVE PLANTS

To keep invasive plants from taking over your garden, bury 6-inch-wide black plastic lawn edging in a complete circle around the plant(s) you want to contain. Be sure to bury it deep enough so you cannot see it.

COLORFUL COMPLEMENTS

Tuck perennial cornflower amid tough neighbors that can hold their own. Bee balm flowers later than perennial cornflower, providing color when other plants are past their peak bloom.

Daylilies are great companions, too. Consider especially the pale yellow varieties such as 'Hyperion', an old classic. 'Happy Returns', an offspring of 'Stella de Oro', is a most agreeable pale yellow that looks particularly pretty with cornflower blue.

Red Valerian
Centranthus ruber

Zones: 5–8

Bloom Time: Early summer to late fall

Light: Full sun

Height: 36 in.

Interest: Showy red, pink, or white, lightly fragrant flowers; attractive grayish green leaves

Red valerian is a fine border plant with clusters of red, deep pink, rose-pink, or pure white, lightly fragrant flowers that top willowlike, gray-green leaves. It starts flowering in late spring and repeats all summer and into fall, even sporadically through the winter in California, especially if spent flowers are removed promptly. Red valerian adds a colorful note to a vase of cut flowers.

How to Grow

Red valerian, a Mediterranean native, fares best in well-drained soil in full sun. It tolerates drought but not shade—there its growth is poor and it doesn't flower well. Plant red valerian in spring from container-grown specimens. Plants respond to cutting by producing more flowers, making this an excellent choice for the cutting garden. Deadhead frequently to encourage more blossoms and to prevent unwanted seedlings of different hues than the parent plant. Propagate from seeds in early spring in a heated greenhouse or simply buy starter plants from your local nursery.

WHERE TO GROW

Plant red valerian in a sunny border next to white- or blue-flowered plants such as delphiniums and columbines, with gray-foliaged artemisias, or in front of shrubs with purple or bronze foliage such as smoke tree or weigela. This plant is equally at home in the Northeast and the Northwest, but not in the Deep South where hot, muggy nights take their toll.

Top Choices

- C. 'Albus', white valerian, is a white sibling. It looks best interplanted with the red form.

- C. 'Coccineus' grows to 36 inches tall with rose-colored flowers from summer to fall.

- C. 'Roseus' bears magenta flowers on 24- to 36-inch-tall stems.

- C. 'Snowcloud' features blossoms of pure white.

TAKING CUTTINGS

Seedlings may produce unwanted flower colors. To produce plants with more uniform flower color, use the following procedure, also appropriate for many other perennials and shrubs:

1 In spring, cut shoots (stem cuttings) from the base of the plants when they are 3 to 4 inches high; make sure to cut the shoot off close to its original stem.

2 Prepare some sandy soil in an area that doesn't get any direct sun, but has bright light.

3 Stick the cuttings in just deep enough so that they stay upright; water gently and cover with a large glass jar. Check every two to three days to make sure leaves don't rot.

4 After six to seven weeks, gradually allow air under the glass jar by propping up one side. Remove the jar completely in another two to three weeks, and transplant cuttings a month later.

THREADLEAF COREOPSIS
Coreopsis verticillata

Zones: 3–9

Bloom Time: Mid-summer until frost

Light: Full sun in the North; light shade in the South

Height: 24–36 in.

Interest: Lacy green foliage topped with myriad bright yellow flowers

Threadleaf coreopsis is noted for its yellow (but sometimes pink) flowers that appear in prodigious quantities all summer. It is indispensable in the garden and looks its best planted in sweeps of ten or more (you simply can't have too many). Its colors blend well with every other color in the rainbow, and the foliage is neat and tidy. Threadleaf coreopsis is a thoroughly well-behaved perennial, deserving of a reputation as one of the world's great garden plants. It has one minor flaw: a tendency to spread a little too freely in climates that remain warm and moist all summer.

HOW TO GROW

Threadleaf coreopsis is very easy to grow. It is drought-tolerant and grows well in sandy soils, but it fares less well in heavy, wet ones. Feed with a low-nitrogen plant food immediately after the first flush of flowers has been cut back. Divide after two to three years. Propagate by rooting summer cuttings taken from nonflowering stems (see page 37).

WHERE TO GROW

Without qualification, threadleaf coreopsis belongs in every perennial bed or mixed border; it is that good. It adds lots of color to plantings of ornamental grasses, especially those whose main show is in fall when they blossom. Although it blooms most heavily in full sun, in the South coreopsis needs light shade. It's also useful as a ground cover since its dense habit will choke out all but the most persistent of weeds. Coreopsis adds consistent color to shrub plantings, most of which bloom in spring. It's nigh impossible to plant it with a color with which it clashes.

Top Choices

- C. 'Grandiflora' has bright golden yellow blossoms on 24- to 30-inch plants.

- C. 'Moonbeam' has cream-yellow flowers on 18-inch-tall stems.

- C. 'Zagreb' grows to only 15 inches tall. Flowers are a deep yellow.

- C. rosea, pink coreopsis, has 1-inch bright pink blossoms on 15-inch plants that bloom all summer and tolerate heavy soils.

SHEARING FOR GROWTH

Shear coreopsis plants after the first flush of flowers to encourage new growth and more abundant repeat blooming. Cut below the faded flowers, leaving lots of leaves on the stems. If you don't shear coreopsis, the plants will flower again, but not as freely.

TRY CAMOUFLAGE

To give an early show of color to perennials whose foliage fills out late, such as Coreopsis 'Moonbeam', underplant with spring-flowering bulbs such as crocuses, dwarf narcissi, grape hyacinths, and species tulips. Their presence prevents accidental damage to the crowns of perennials from overenthusiastic cultivation. The perennial foliage will hide unattractive bulb foliage as it goes dormant in summer.

DELPHINIUM
Delphinium

Zones: 3–8

Bloom Time: Summer

Light: Full sun

Height: 48–60 in.

Interest: Light blue spikes on tall plants

Delphinium is one of the great plants of Europe. The *belladonna* types grow 4 to 5 feet tall and are the most durable varieties available (lasting three to four years) for American gardeners. They come in an assortment of blue, purple, and white shades, but lack the grandeur of the more stately delphiniums of European gardens. The *elatum* hybrids, while long-lasting perennials in Europe, perform brilliantly in American gardens for just a year or two. This makes them magnificent, if somewhat expensive, annuals or biennials. They're worth trying, though, especially in northern and coastal gardens.

HOW TO GROW
Delphiniums require soil that retains moisture but never becomes waterlogged (especially in winter). They are heavy feeders, succeeding best where the soil is deeply

cultivated with lots of added organic matter. Apply a low-nitrogen fertilizer liberally in early spring. Staking is essential (see page 81). Cut the spikes back to the top of the foliage after blossoming for repeat blooms in late summer and early fall.

WHERE TO GROW

Delphiniums must have full sun and should be planted at the back of the perennial border. They resent the heat and humidity of the Southeast, succeeding best where nights cool down. They are magnificent as cut flowers, providing height, color, and drama in mixed bouquets.

Top Choices

- *D.* x *belladonna* 'Bellamosum' is similar to the parent species except that it has rich, dark blue flowers.

- *D.* x *b.* 'Casa Blanca' is a pure white selection.

- *D. elatum* hybrids include the well-known Round Table series, which grow to 6 or 7 feet. Plant in fall so that they are well established when spring rolls around. 'Astolat' is a lovely lavender-pink with a black or gold center; 'Black Knight' is the darkest violet with a black center; 'Blue Bird' is sky blue with a white center; 'Galahad' is pure white; and 'King Arthur' is dark royal violet with a white center.

FLOWERS FOR CUTTING

When your perennial border is in full flower, it is often tempting to snip a few of the brightest blooms for an enticing indoor arrangement. Every blossom picked for the vase means one less in the garden, often leaving holes in the overall view of your flower bed. To keep it in colorful bloom and your house in full flower, too, consider planting a colorful cutting garden.

Also called a flower arranger's garden, a cutting garden can be part of the vegetable patch or a garden all to itself, but probably out of prominent view—so you can cut its blooms to use to your heart's content.

For beautiful bouquets from your cutting garden, plant perennials with bright, long-lasting flowers or colorful foliage on sturdy stems. In addition to plants featured in this book, consider including baby's-breath for filler, lilies for added drama, and a variety of your favorite annuals to expand your color palette.

When arranging the bounty from your garden in a container, be sure to strip the leaves from the portion of the stalk that will be in water. Adding an aspirin to the water and changing the water regularly will also help keep your bouquets looking fresh.

GARDEN PINK
Dianthus 'Bath's Pink'

Zones: 4–8

Bloom Time: Summer

Light: Full sun

Height: 8–10 in.

Interest: Masses of fragrant, fringed, single, pink blossoms that appear in early summer; repeat blooms until late summer

In early summer, 'Bath's Pink' produces lots of fragrant, single, pink flowers that have a darker ring around their centers. Considered one of the best varieties of garden pink, it continues to throw blossoms until late in the growing season. 'Bath's Pink' was discovered growing in an old garden in Georgia and was derived from the European Cheddar pink. It thrives, of course, in the Deep South but also flourishes in the North's much colder climates. The blossoms have the sweet scent of cloves and appear on wiry stems above grassy, blue-green foliage.

HOW TO GROW
All garden pinks are not too fussy about soil conditions, but they do require good drainage. They will grow with abandon in any reasonable garden soil, and 'Bath's Pink' in particular will tolerate heat and humidity.

Deadheading (see page 23) encourages even more blossoms. Because this, like other garden pinks, prefers a pH close to neutral, give it a yearly handful of ground dolomitic limestone everywhere but in alkaline regions of the country.

WHERE TO GROW

This adaptable plant will tolerate a wide variety of growing conditions, so it allows many options for garden placement. It is equally at home at the edge of a garden border, along paths, in pockets in a dry stone wall, in rock gardens, on dry sunny banks, and in containers.

Top Choices

- *D.* x *allwoodii* 'Alpinus' is a lively strain of 6- to 8-inch hybrids with lacy-edged flowers in a wide variety of pinks, reds, and whites. Most have contrasting "eyes" around their centers; all have that delicious clove fragrance.

- *D.* 'Doris', the best-known double-flowered garden pink, has blossoms of light salmon pink accented with a crimson ring. The 12-inch plants bloom for weeks starting in early summer.

- *D. gratianopolitanus* 'Tiny Rubies' is a delightful miniature with a galaxy of tiny, deep pink, double flowers that look like baby carnations on 4-inch stems.

Garden Companions

With its soft colors and low habit, garden pink blends easily with both low, creeping plants and taller flowers including:

- BLEEDING-HEART
- CREEPING THYME
- DELPHINIUMS
- LAMB'S-EARS
- PEACHLEAF BELLFLOWER
- PERENNIAL DUSTY-MILLER
- PERENNIAL FOXGLOVE
- PERENNIAL GERANIUMS
- SNOW-IN-SUMMER

MAXIMUM FRAGRANCE

If spicy fragrance is what you want, the hybrid 18-inch 'Rainbow Loveliness' is the garden pink for your sunny border. Its lacy flowers have delicate, deeply cut petals in a range of pinks, plus a very strong, clovelike perfume. The scent is as delicious as dessert.

PERENNIAL FOXGLOVE
Digitalis grandiflora

Zones: 4–8

Bloom Time: Early summer, with repeat bloom until fall

Light: Full to part sun

Height: 30–36 in.

Interest: Pale yellow flowers

Perennial foxglove (also known by the botanical name *D. ambigua*) is one of the few truly perennial foxgloves. Most other foxgloves are biennial—they produce leaves one year, flower the next, produce seeds, then die. Perennial foxglove, on the other hand, lasts in the garden for years. In mild climates, its foliage is evergreen. The pale yellow spikes blend well with almost every other shade, so it's easy to combine it with other plants. Like its shorter-lived relatives, it makes an excellent cut flower; for best results, cut stems when about half their buds have opened.

HOW TO GROW
Foxglove requires moist (not wet) soils and resents drying out. To ensure these conditions, apply liberal quantities of organic matter to the soil before planting and

again in spring before plants are in active growth. The only maintenance required is to remove the dead flower spikes. Do this as the flowers are spent and before the plants put energy into seed production. Remember to leave a few seedpods if you want more plants.

WHERE TO GROW

Perennial foxglove is a versatile plant that tolerates both full sun and part shade. The pale yellow flowers look best when planted next to hot-colored flowers; they manage to get your attention without making a scene. Perennial foxglove is equally at home in a formal perennial garden, mixed border, or naturalized woodland setting.

Top Choices

- *D. lanata,* Grecian foxglove, has unusual fawn-colored blossoms with purple veins and an almost white lip. The dense spikes grow 30 to 36 inches tall. This is a biennial that sometimes grows as a perennial.

- *D. purpurea* 'Excelsior Hybrids' are biennial hybrid foxgloves that have huge flower spikes with pink, red, or white florets that appear all around the 5- to 7-foot stems. 'Foxy' is similar but grows to 3 feet.

- *D.* x *mertonensis* has incredible strawberry red flowers on 36- to 48-inch spikes. Perennial in Zones 6 to 8; best treated as a biennial in Zones 4 and 5.

AVOIDING THE BURN

In northern climates, plants with evergreen foliage such as perennial foxglove are usually "burned" by arctic blasts of wind. Plants that die back can also be damaged by alternate freezing and thawing. To reduce this damage:

1️⃣ Lay evergreen branches over the crowns in late November.

2️⃣ To protect the plants even further, lay straw around (not over) the crowns before laying down the branches.

3️⃣ Remove winter protection about the time the forsythia blooms in your area.

CAUTION:

Keep foxglove away from children. All types of foxglove are toxic if eaten. Educate children about all plants, including foxglove, and warn them not to put any part of any plant in their mouths unless told it is safe.

PURPLE CONEFLOWER
Echinacea purpurea

Zones: 4–9

Bloom Time: June to frost

Light: Full to part sun

Height: 24–40 in.

Interest: Very large rose, pink, or white daisies; loved by butterflies

This North American native, closely related to black-eyed Susan, is a must for the perennial border. A great garden plant, purple coneflower has brightly colored blossoms in shades of purplish red, rosy pink, carmine, or crimson red—depending on how you see color. Pure white selections provide an interesting contrast when planted with the brighter shades. Purple coneflower has a contrasting center that starts as a dark brown disk, gradually turns orange, swells to become cone shaped, and finally turns black as the seeds mature. Flowers start blooming in June above dark green foliage and continue until frost. All summer, clouds of butterflies find the blossoms irresistible. Coneflowers are a wonderful addition to summer bouquets; after the petals have fallen, the cones are a nice addition to dried arrangements.

HOW TO GROW

Purple coneflower grows well in average garden soils or in hot, dry conditions, but it resents wet feet. It is equally happy in either full or part sun and requires only deadheading to keep it blooming vigorously and to keep it tidy. It will self-sow, with seedlings usually varying in shade from the parent plant but attractive nonetheless. The plants never require staking, but they are prey to Japanese beetles. (See page 79 for ways to control this pest.) In the South, divide the plant crowns every three to four years to keep purple coneflower vigorous.

WHERE TO GROW

Purple coneflower belongs in every perennial border and cutting garden, in meadows, or planted alongside liatris and butterfly bush in a garden for butterflies and summer color. The brightly colored flowers and the butterflies the flowers attract make them great plants for children to grow.

Top Choices

- *E.* 'Bravado' has large rose-colored flowers with deep maroon centers.

- *E.* 'Bright Star' has rosy pink flowers on 30- to 40-inch-tall spikes.

- *E.* 'Crimson Star' has bright crimsonred flowers that are fairly flat.

- *E.* 'Magnus' bears bright carmine rose flowers on 36- to 42-inch stalks.

- *E.* 'White Swan' produces pure white blossoms on 36- to 40-inch stalks.

MEADOW GARDENING

A meadow garden is an area in full sun where native and introduced plants are used to create the look of a field that has not been cultivated. Natural meadows achieve balance between grasses, wildflowers, and woody plants. Woody plants must be cut back periodically to avoid ending up with a "woods."

In North America, examples are unplowed prairies and areas above the tree line in mountainous regions. Eastern prairies are usually called meadows or fields.

Seedlings will be smothered by perennial weeds unless you are willing to spend a few years weeding diligently. To start a meadow:

1 Cultivate the soil as if you were developing a perennial border.

2 Remove all undesirable vegetation and add organic matter and fertilizer to the soil. If possible, leave the area bare for six weeks so weed seeds can sprout and be removed before you plant your meadow.

3 Plant the species you want in the meadow from transplants, or sow a meadow wildflower mixture suitable for your area.

4 Keep out weeds until desirable plants are well established. A once-a-year mowing in fall will take care of controlling unwanted tree and shrub seedlings.

GLOBE THISTLE
Echinops ritro

Zones: 3–10

Bloom Time: Mid- to late summer

Light: Full sun

Height: 2–4 ft.

Interest: Unique round, steel blue flower heads; dramatic foliage

Globe thistle, with its prickly personality, will never gain stardom in the border, but this European native does provide a steel blue color and round shape found in no other flower. It is excellent for fresh flower arrangements and very enticing to honeybees and moths. The attractive foliage is not as daunting as the plant's common name would suggest—globe is not a true thistle, just a good imitator. It is a tough, no-nonsense perennial that grows almost anywhere.

HOW TO GROW

Globe thistle prefers full sun and average to rich, well-drained garden soil. It is very drought-tolerant and can thrive in conditions that would wilt other perennials. Taller varieties need staking in windy locations and excessively fertile soil. They are very long-lasting, low maintenance plants. Propagate from seeds, or root cuttings, or by division.

WHERE TO GROW

Plant globe thistle at the back or in the middle of a mixed border, where its unusual color and flower shape will provide an interesting contrast to other perennials. Globe thistle is also useful in meadow gardens, where it will thrive for years with little or no attention. Plant it in front of tall grasses for a backdrop for its unusual flowers, or combine it with other summer bloomers such as daylilies, purple coneflower, bee balm, and phlox.

Top Choices

- *E.* 'Taplow Blue' has bright metallic blue flowers on 3- to 4-foot stalks.

- *E.* 'Veitch's Blue' bears dark blue flowers on 36- to 40-inch stalks. Flowers are somewhat smaller but more abundant.

- *E. exaltatus* has white to grayish blue flowers and grows 4 to 6 feet high.

ROOT CUTTINGS

When stem cuttings are not possible, use root cuttings to get new plants exactly like the parent. Plants to propagate in this manner include phlox, sea holly, globe thistle, and Oriental poppies.

1 In midfall, fill a flowerpot with a rooting medium that is two parts pasteurized potting soil, one part coarse sand. Press evenly to firm the soil.

2 Carefully dig up the plant and choose no more than one-third of the thickest roots. With a very sharp knife, cut off the roots close to the crown of the plant. Take care to keep the ends closest to the crown together, as new shoots arise only from this "top" end.

3 Cut the roots into 2- to 3-inch lengths—arranging so the root tops all face the same direction.

4 Make a hole that is large enough to insert each root piece upright ("top" end up) in the rooting medium without bending or snapping it.

5 Water and place the container in a temperature of 45° to 55° F. No light is needed until new shoots begin to push up through the soil.

6 In spring, separate the new plants and plant them in the garden. Protect from direct sunlight for a week.

SEA HOLLY

Eryngium amethystinum

Zones: 5–10

Bloom Time: Mid-summer

Light: Full sun

Height: 36 in.

Interest: Masses of amethyst-blue, teasel-like flowers that are lovely fresh or dried

Sea holly is a uniquely beautiful ornamental plant with blossoms, bracts, and stems a striking shade of amethyst blue. Teasel-like flowers are produced in prodigious quantities. They are long-lasting in fresh bouquets and fine in dried arrangements. There is much confusion about the names of the various sea hollies, as they are somewhat promiscuous, but all the progeny are attractive and should not be ignored simply because they lack a pedigree. Plants propagated vegetatively (by root cuttings) are identical to the parent. Seed-grown plants may not be.

HOW TO GROW

Sea holly is easy to grow in full sun and is tolerant of most soils except wet ones. Staking and deadheading are never needed, so this plant is really low maintenance and is almost pest-free. Dividing sea holly is somewhat tricky because of its taproot; divide in spring for best results. It is easiest to propagate plants from root cuttings (see page 49).

WHERE TO GROW

Ironically, in spite of its name, sea holly prefers locations in full sun with average to dry soil. It tolerates drought and shrugs off saltwater spray, making it ideal for coastal gardens.

Top Choices

- *E. alpinum*, alpine sea holly, has blue conelike flowers with steel blue bracts and grows 24 to 30 inches high.

- *E. giganteum* 'Miss Willmott's Ghost', giant sea holly, is a biennial that self-sows freely, with seedlings popping up in the most surprising of places. It has large, silver gray flowers on 30- to 36-inch-high plants.

- *E. bourgatii*, Moroccan or Mediterranean sea holly, has striking blue and green flowers on an 18- to 24-inch plant. The foliage is white veined and handsome.

- *E. planum*, flat sea holly, has numerous silvery blue blooms on 24- to 36-inch-tall plants. The variety 'Blue Cap' is the best sea holly for the South.

Garden Companions

Grow sea holly in the middle or the front of a mixed border, planted beside strong-colored plants or those with white flowers or silvery gray foliage. Its bold form and texture add wonderful contrast to garden settings. Good choices include:

- BABY'S-BREATH
- BLUESTAR
- DAYLILIES
- GARDEN PHLOX
- LAMB'S-EARS
- PERENNIAL DUSTY-MILLER
- PERENNIAL GERANIUMS
- PURPLE SAGE

PERENNIALS FOR
SEASIDE GARDENS

The salt spray, ever-present breezes, and sandy soil of coastal locations present a challenge to perennial gardeners. Tough but beautiful plants that enjoy seaside garden locations include bee balm, butterfly weed, columbine, daylilies, false indigo, globe thistle, Oriental poppy, phlox, and perennial dusty-miller.

HARDY AGERATUM
Eupatorium coelestinum

Zones: 5–10

Bloom Time: Late summer

Light: Full to part sun

Height: 20–24 in.

Interest: Clouds of light or lavender-blue flowers

Hardy ageratum adds a sparkle to the late-summer border when many other perennials have passed their peak. This native of the eastern United States is not a true ageratum (those are annuals), but its pale lavender-blue color is identical to its annual namesake. The garden effect of hardy ageratum is similar to that of the annual forms, and you don't have the chore of replanting it every year. Because of the so-called "ageratum effect," it is difficult to reproduce the exact color of these flowers in print. What the human eye sees, beautiful light blue flowers, is different from what photographic film records, pink blossoms. Hardy ageratum makes a superb cut flower and is also a magnet for butterflies; one of the joys of the late-summer garden is seeing scores of brightly colored butterflies landing on the lavender-blue blossoms.

HOW TO GROW

Hardy ageratum prefers evenly moist soil—not too wet and not too dry—and it flowers equally well in full sun or part shade. Propagate by division in early spring. Shear it to half its size in early July to reduce the need for staking. If you prefer the plant to reach its full size, place brushwood all around and among the crowns in late spring to prevent it from falling over. Keep it well mulched (not over the crowns, though). Water well with soaker hoses during warm, dry spells.

WHERE TO GROW

Hardy ageratum belongs at the front of the border in an area that allows it room to grow. Unless checked by vigorous neighbors, it spreads quickly without being invasive. Plant enough so you can use these delightful, fluffy flowers in late-summer arrangements.

Top Choices

- *E.* 'Cori' has deep lavender-blue flowers on 24-inch-tall stems.

- *E. maculatum,* Joe-Pye weed, is a native plant with pink flowers on 4- to 6-foot stems; it likes moist to damp soil. 'Gateway' is the best form available, with huge, reddish purple flower heads that turn a shade of dark chocolate as they mature. It is much loved by butterflies. Zones 4 to 7.

- *E. purpureum,* another Joe-Pye weed, is taller than the above but also likes very moist soil. It has very large, rosy purple flower heads in late summer and early fall.

Garden Companions

Hardy ageratum is most effective planted with late-summer to early-fall bloomers, including any of these selections:

- BLACK-EYED SUSAN
- BOLTONIA
- CALAMINT
- LAMB'S-EARS
- LIATRIS
- NEW ENGLAND ASTER
- RUSSIAN SAGE
- SEDUM 'AUTUMN JOY'
- STOKES' ASTER
- WHITE OBEDIENT PLANT

PLACING SUBTLY COLORED FLOWERS

Plants that flower in gentle colors, such as the hardy ageratum, look best beside other subtle shades. White-flowered plants make good companions, as do those with blooms of any non-flashy hue and those with gray or blue foliage.

QUEEN-OF-THE-PRAIRIE
Filipendula rubra

Zones: 3–8

Bloom Time: Early summer

Light: Full to part sun

Height: 60–72 in.

Interest: Plumes of tiny blossoms reminiscent of cotton candy

Queen-of-the-prairie is a rugged individual from the American prairie that has been cultivated for centuries in gardens both here and in Europe. This statuesque, native plant makes its presence known in the summer border with its frothy pink plumes atop stems up to 6 feet tall.

HOW TO GROW

Queen-of-the-prairie is happiest in rich, moist, evenly damp soil; in dry conditions, it produces shorter, weaker stems. Mulch well to hold in moisture, and water thoroughly during dry summer weather. It prefers soil with a pH close to neutral, i.e. one that is neither acidic nor alkaline. In full sun, it is impervious to wind and requires no staking. While queen-of-the-prairie flowers well in part shade, it needs support for the top-heavy blossoms (in the South, part shade is required). To propagate, divide the crowns in spring before growth begins or in fall as the plants go dormant.

WHERE TO GROW

Queen-of-the-prairie makes a bold statement wherever it is planted. It is often used as an accent plant at the back of a border or in the center of an island bed. It is also striking when planted near a stream or pond (not in the water), where constant moisture encourages the plants to develop into dramatic specimens. Combine queen-of-the-prairie with shorter plants to emphasize its stature. It can hold its own planted with other tall perennials and even with shrubs.

Top Choices

- *F.* 'Venusta' has larger and deeper pink flowers. 'Venusta' is also known as Martha Washington's plume; it is assumed that it was grown in the gardens of Mount Vernon.

- *F. purpurea* 'Elegans' grows 18 to 24 inches tall with large, rough-textured leaves and clouds of pale pink flowers. Zones 4 to 8.

- *F. p.* 'Nana' is a real sweetheart with pink flowers on compact 12-inch-tall stems. Zones 4 to 8.

- *F. vulgaris,* dropwort, has creamy white flowers on 2- to 3-foot stems, with a dome of delicately cut, fernlike leaves. 'Flore Pleno' is a double-flowered selection with larger white blossoms.

ISLAND BEDS

An island bed is a garden that you can walk around, in contrast to a one-sided border that is usually backed up to a wall, fence, or hedge. One of the advantages of island beds is that plants can be seen from all sides. In addition, they do not develop into single-sided plants as they sometimes do in a one-sided border.

The easiest way to design an island bed is to use a flexible garden hose to form a pleasing, irregular, curved shape on bare ground or lawn in the desired location.

If the bed is located in a lawn, remove and discard the grass. On any site, loosen the soil to a depth of 12 inches, and work in lots of compost or other organic matter.

Plant perennials such as queen-of-the-prairies, hollyhocks, perennial sunflowers, or delphiniums in the center of an island bed. Position lower-growing perennials at the edges.

BLANKET FLOWER

Gaillardia x *grandiflora*

Zones: Zones 3–10

Bloom Time: Summer into fall

Light: Full sun

Height: 24–36 in.

Interest: Masses of gaily colored, daisylike flowers

When other plants buckle under to heat and humidity, blanket flower continues to shine—even in the South, where other plants take a siesta when the temperatures rise. North or South, this plant is easy to grow and produces lots of brightly colored flowers that last a long time in both garden and vase. The blossoms can be single or semidouble and appear in shades of yellow and red, or in bands of both on the same flower.

HOW TO GROW

Blanket flower requires full sun and a light, well-drained soil that is low in nutrients. Avoid fertilizers, or the plants will produce lush foliage that is more susceptible to rot. Deadheading, a necessary chore for most plants, is usually not needed to keep the plants blooming. Blanket flower tends to be short-lived in the garden, especially in the South. It is easy to propagate by division or from seeds, and starter plants are relatively inexpensive at garden centers.

WHERE TO GROW

Blanket flower is as versatile as it is colorful. Given a prominent spot in the perennial border, this vibrant gem will produce an eye-catching display all summer long. Its proclivity for blooming also makes it an invaluable plant in dry meadows. Plant enough to use for floral arrangements, too. You'll find blanket flower used extensively in wildflower seed mixtures for naturalizing.

Top Choices

- G. 'Baby Cole' grows 6 to 8 inches tall with red flowers tipped with yellow.

- G. 'Burgundy' has large, wine red blooms on 2- to 3-foot plants.

- G. 'Goblin' has large flowers with red petals and yellow edges; it grows 9 to 12 inches tall.

- G. 'The Sun' is 15 inches tall with pure golden yellow flowers.

Garden Companions

Blanket flower's bright colors go well with plants that act as a background as well as those that soften its bold presence.

- BABY'S-BREATH
- BLUE OAT GRASS
- DELPHINIUMS
- GARDEN PHLOX
- PEACHLEAF BELLFLOWER
- PERENNIAL DUSTY-MILLER
- SEA HOLLY
- WHITE CONEFLOWER
- YARROWS

GROWING
FROM SEEDS

It is very easy and rewarding to grow blanket flower from seeds. Moisten a flat of seed starter, then mix and scatter the seeds over the soil. Do not cover, as these seeds need light to germinate. Instead, loosely cover the flat with clear plastic wrap; place in a warm location with indirect light. Seedlings should begin to emerge in about three weeks.

PERENNIAL GERANIUM
Geranium

Zones: 4–7

Bloom Time: Early summer to fall

Light: Full sun to light shade

Height: 15–18 in.

Interest: Masses of pink or blue blossoms; attractive, lacy leaves

Perennial geranium, also known as cranesbill, has a strong personality for a small plant, perhaps the reason for its reputation as a must-have plant for gardeners everywhere. When in bloom, it virtually covers itself with striking blue or pink flowers. The blooms are set off with pleasing bright green, deeply divided leaves. *NOTE:* Perennial geraniums are not to be confused with *Pelargonium*—the ubiquitous pot geranium with spheres of brilliant red or pink flowers.

HOW TO GROW
Perennial geranium is generally easy to grow and thrives in ordinary, well-drained, fertile soil. In the North it prefers full sun, but in the heat and humidity of the South it requires protection from afternoon sun. (High shade from trees is ideal.) It is virtually pest- and disease-free,

which is always a blessing. If the plants become straggly after flowering, as they often do in part shade, cut them back to the new foliage.

WHERE TO GROW

Place perennial geranium in a prominent location at the front of a border, surrounded by more subtle shades that complement its show-off personality. It can also be used as a ground cover between shrubs such as bridal-wreath spirea, but allow plenty of space between the shrubs so the geraniums are not heavily shaded.

Top Choices

- G. *clarkei* 'Kashmir White' has lots of white 1-inch blooms on sturdy 15- to 20-inch plants.

- G. *endressii* 'Wargrave Pink' is a vigorous grower to 18 inches tall, with a loose, but not unpleasant, sprawling habit. Flowers are a very pleasant shade of pink.

- G. 'Johnson's Blue' has violet-blue blossoms on 12- to 24-inch plants. It produces abundant flowers in May and June and is virtually carefree.

- G. *sanguineum*, the so-called bloody cranesbill, is covered with masses of carmine red flowers over a long period. The 15- to 18-inch plants spread 24 to 36 inches. 'Alpenglow' is an especially nice selection. The variety *striatum* is more compact with pale pink blooms.

ARMENIAN CRANESBILL

Armenian cranesbill, *Geranium psilostemon,* is a plant for gardens with lots of space and lots of spirit—space because this is a large, spreading plant that needs room to grow; spirit because its flowers are a strong rosy purple. For those who enjoy the challenge of planting with a strong palette, Armenian cranesbill is a real winner.

Armenian cranesbill, which reaches 36 to 48 inches tall, is easy to grow and blooms all summer. With colorful flowers and attractive maplelike foliage on branching stems, it certainly draws attention to your garden.

This showy plant thrives in well-drained, fertile soil. In the North, it prefers full sun; in the heat and humidity of the South, protection from afternoon sun (ideally with high shade from trees) is a must. Armenian cranesbill is virtually pest- and disease-free. It may require some staking.

SNEEZEWEED
Helenium autumnale

Zones: 3–10

Bloom Time: Late summer to early fall

Light: Full sun

Height: 48–60 in.

Interest: Masses of autumn-colored flowers

Sneezeweed is a valuable addition to the mixed border because its bloom time comes after most perennials have given up for the year. The flowers, in glowing autumn shades of yellow, red, and bronze, appear on strong, stiffly upright stems and are ideal for cutting. They also provide food for butterflies on their southerly migration. Despite its common name, sneezeweed does not cause sneezing. Hybridizers have combined the hardiness of this eastern species with the larger, brighter colored flowers of western species to produce many vividly colored selections.

HOW TO GROW
Sneezeweed prefers full sun in evenly moist soil but will tolerate wet areas. If your soil tends to dry out, water often and add lots of organic matter such as leaf mold

or well-rotted compost to retain moisture. Taller varieties require staking unless you cut the stems back to half their height in late June. The shorter plants will grow bushier and produce even more flowers. To propagate, divide plants in early spring just as the new shoots appear.

WHERE TO GROW

Plant sneezeweed toward the middle or back of a mixed border. It is especially useful for filling in after spring-flowering perennials, such as bleeding-heart, have declined. Sneezeweed is an excellent cut flower, providing abundant color in floral arrangements.

Top Choices

- *H.* 'Brilliant' lives up to its name with an abundance of fiery-colored flowers from mid- to late summer on 36-inch stems.

- *H.* 'Butterpat' has yellow flowers and grows 3 to 4 feet tall.

- *H.* 'Moerheim Beauty' bears bold, deep red flowers that fade to antique gold as they age; stems are 36 inches.

- *H.* 'Riverton Beauty' is an old selection with deep brown centers in the golden yellow blossoms.

AVOIDING STAKES

To avoid staking sneezeweed and similar tall-growing plants that flower in late summer, cut them down to half their height around the Fourth of July. Cutting them down before flowering will make plants bushier and less prone to flopping over.

FOR ABUNDANT FLOWERING

To ensure lots of sneezeweed flowers for the longest time possible during the summer, be sure to:

- Keep soil evenly moist.

- Deadhead regularly. Once plants begin to blossom, remove faded flowers as soon as they begin to go by. This helps stimulate the formation of more flower buds.

PERENNIAL SUNFLOWER
Helianthus x *multiflorus*

Zones: 4–10

Bloom Time: Mid- to late summer

Light: Full sun (part shade in the South)

Height: 48–60 in.

Interest: Lots of long-lasting blooms

Bushy, bright green foliage makes a perfect foil for the masses of golden yellow blossoms characteristic of the showy perennial sunflower. This bold plant adds a clear, cheery note to any border or vase. Perennial sunflower is a very tall hybrid that is well-mannered in the border, growing vigorously but not invasively. Its relatives include the much-loved and useful annual sunflower (*H. annuus*) and Jerusalem artichoke (*H. tuberosus*), which is a confusing colloquial name for this North American sunflower.

HOW TO GROW
Perennial sunflower does best in regularly fertilized soil (spring and fall) amended with organic matter, such as rotted manure. After flowering is complete, cut plants back to the ground. It likes soil that doesn't dry out too

much in summer; water during rainless spells. In the North and West this sunflower prefers full sun; in the South it appreciates some shade, though if it's too dark stems will need staking. Pinch growing tips in mid-June (late May in the South) to increase branching and reduce the need for staking.

WHERE TO GROW

Perennial sunflower is a big plant that needs ample room to grow. Group several at the back of a mixed shrub and perennial border, or use as a screen to block an unsightly view or provide privacy during summer. A group of three or more is also ideal located in the center of a large island bed.

Top Choices

- *H.* 'Capenock Star' has single, yellow flowers with golden brown centers.

- *H.* 'Flore-Pleno' bears double, bright yellow blooms that resemble small dahlias.

- *H.* 'Loddon Gold' has larger, bright yellow, double blooms and taller stems than other varieties.

- *H. angustifolius,* swamp sunflower, has narrow, willowlike, dark green leaves on 5- to 8-foot plants with abundant 2- to 3-inch, yellow, daisy-like flowers in autumn. Zones 6 to 9.

Garden Companions

Perennial sunflowers are excellent companions to other tall, late-blooming plants, including:

- BEE BALM
- CROCOSMIAS
- CULVER'S ROOT
- GLOBE THISTLE
- HOLLYHOCK MALLOW
- JAPANESE ANEMONE
- ORIENTAL LILIES
- TALL DAHLIAS
- TALL ORNAMENTAL GRASSES
- RUSSIAN SAGE

FOR THE BIRDS

If allowed to go to seed, perennial sunflowers produce food for many birds. If this is your goal, don't cut plants to the ground after flowering.

Cardinals, purple finches, nuthatches, chickadees, and slate-colored juncos are especially attracted to sunflowers. If you are a bird lover, plant your sunflowers outside a window to give yourself an unobstructed view of these cheery flowers and the birds they attract.

FALSE SUNFLOWER

Heliopsis helianthoides

Zones: 4–9

Bloom Time: Mid-summer to fall

Light: Full sun

Height: 48–60 in.

Interest: Prolific, relatively large golden or yellow blossoms

This North American native perennial closely resembles perennial sunflower and produces a fine show of 3- to 4-inch yellow or yellowish orange daisies for most of the summer. The blossoms of false sunflower are either single, semidouble (with petals surrounding the dark centers), or fully double (completely concealing the center). This plant has found a well-deserved home in perennial borders around the world because it is so free-flowering and trouble-free. As a cut flower, it is long-lasting and always perky.

HOW TO GROW

False sunflower tolerates drier soils than perennial sunflower and requires little in the way of fertilizing. Plants require staking unless they're cut back to half their height in mid-June. Regular deadheading increases the amount of blooms and decreases the number of volunteer seedlings. The only other required care is to cut the plants to the ground after frost has ended their blooming season.

WHERE TO GROW

False sunflower is a tidy, well-behaved plant that fits into any perennial or mixed border. It can be used as a specimen plant among shorter perennials or amid taller neighbors such as ornamental grasses or shrubs. It is superb when cut for use in summer and fall floral arrangements.

Top Choices

- *H.* 'Golden Plume' grows 4 feet tall with semidouble to double, 3-inch blooms in a lovely deep yellow shade.

- *H.* 'Karat' grows to 4 feet with huge, single, bright yellow blossoms.

- *H.* 'Summer Sun' is usually grown from seeds and is somewhat variable. The golden yellow flowers are single or double and appear on 36- to 48-inch-tall plants. 'Summer Sun' is especially heat-tolerant.

MANAGING GARDEN GOLD

Many of the plants that blossom from midsummer to early fall bear flowers in vibrant shades of yellow, gold, orange, or red. Just a few of these perennials can brighten the border, but too many planted too closely together will have you gardening in sunglasses. To soften the effect of masses of brightly colored summer flowers:

- Interplant with clumps of ornamental grasses.

- Plant perennials that bear white, blue, or violet flowers such as globe thistle, Russian sage, or white garden phlox between clumps of yellow or gold flowers. Plants with blue-gray to silver foliage are also good softeners.

STRENGTH IN NUMBERS

Tall plants such as false sunflower that are grown in full sun have stronger stems than those grown in part shade. You can support these without staking by planting them in large groups. The sturdy plants then help support each other.

DAYLILY
Hemerocallis

Zones: 3–9

Bloom Time: Summer

Light: Full sun

Height: 24–48 in.

Interest: Brilliant blossoms in myriad hues on tidy, easy care plants

Daylilies are as tough as iron and free of pests; they spread quickly but not aggressively and flower freely. They're not very fussy about growing conditions. Thanks to enthusiastic hybridizers, there are more than thirty thousand varieties in every color but blue. Daylilies are often confused with true lilies, which grow from bulbs and have leaves that clothe the flower stem. In contrast, daylilies have fleshy roots and coarse, grasslike foliage that grows directly from the crown of the plant.

HOW TO GROW
Daylilies tolerate even poor soil as long as it's well drained, but they grow best in good, rich, deeply worked soil. Mulch well and water during rainless spells to ensure flower production throughout dry times. Fertilize in early spring and late fall. One regular chore

remains. Remove each day's spent blossoms to keep plants looking tidy. Each one lasts only a day, hence the Latin name, *Hemerocallis,* meaning "beautiful for a day." Divide in spring or fall if flowering declines.

WHERE TO GROW

Horticulturists consider the daylily one of the backbone plants of a border. Its habit of flowering over a long period makes it invaluable massed in a bed or for use in a mixed planting with other perennials, shrubs, or both. Daylilies make a great ground cover, as their vigorous growth chokes out most weeds. Use them on sunny banks, where their strong roots help hold the soil in place. They can also be naturalized along roadsides and in wild gardens.

Top Choices

- *H.* 'Catherine Woodbury' has pink and cream blooms on 30-inch stems.

- *H.* 'Stella de Oro' grows masses of golden yellow blossoms all summer on plants that grow to 2 feet tall. 'Happy Returns' is an 18-inch tall offspring with all the virtues of the parent, but is a lovely, soft shade of lemon yellow.

- *H.* 'Hyperion' is fragrant, canary yellow, and grows 48 inches high. It is about seventy-five years old, but it's still one of the best performers.

- *H.* 'Pink Lavender Appeal' has beautiful lavender-pink blossoms with green throats on 26-inch plants.

DAYLILY SALAD

Some gardeners believe that nothing is prettier than a mass of daylilies in full bloom in the border. Others believe one thing comes close—daylilies in full bloom in a tossed salad. To enjoy them in your salad bowl:

1 Plant daylily varieties with fragrant lemon yellow flowers. These have the best texture and flavor. Some nice, tasty choices include 'Chartreuse Magic', 'Happy Returns', and 'Hyperion'.

2 Pick the flowers soon after they open and just before serving. Arrange individual petals on salad greens to add color and flavor. Petals are also delightful dipped in a light dressing for a snack.

The pastel yellow flowers of 'Happy Returns' are a wonderful accent to just about everything else in the garden.

JAPANESE IRIS

Iris ensata

Zones: 4–9

Bloom Time: Mid-summer

Light: Full sun

Height: 24–48 in.

Interest: Huge orchid-like blossoms that float like exotic birds above rich green foliage

When it's in bloom, Japanese iris provides one of the most outstanding floral displays a garden can feature. For hundreds of years, specialists in Japan have been hybridizing this plant to produce some of the largest flowers of any perennial (up to 10 inches across), in shades of lavender, maroon, mauve, pink, purple, and white. One of the delights of Japanese iris is that all the subtle variations in hue are perfectly complementary to each other. The long, swordlike foliage remains attractive even after the flowers fade.

HOW TO GROW

Japanese iris has three essential requirements: sun, acidic soil, and abundant moisture. It requires no other care beyond picking off Japanese beetles, which have a fondness for the flowers (see page 79). Divide in late August to give the plants a chance to become well established before winter. Protection is necessary for the first winter in northern climates (see page 45).

WHERE TO GROW

Japanese irises thrive in wet soils, so they're ideal for the edges of ponds or streams. Plant as a delicate accent in a mixed border or in groups by themselves—in a location where you can bask in the full impact of their delightful beauty. Since Japanese irises make astonishing cut flowers, be sure to make room for them in a wet corner of the cutting garden.

Top Choices

- *I.* 'Gold Bound' has snow white, double flowers up to 6 inches across. Each petal is marked with a gold band.

- *I.* 'Emotion' evokes the same with its large white flowers edged in purple.

- *I.* 'Great White Heron' has pure white flowers up to 11 inches across.

- *I.* 'Maroon Giant' has large, ruffled blooms in a velvety, dark red-violet hue.

- *I.* 'Nikko' is a shorter variety than most; its pale lavender-blue flowers are veined in deep purple.

- *I.* 'Pink Frost' has 8-inch, semidouble, fluffy flowers in a shade of near-pink.

- *I.* 'Purple and Gold' is a variety that makes up in drama for what its name lacks in imagination.

ACIDIFYING THE SOIL

Choose from these two options to make soil more acidic:

1 Add at least 6 inches of shredded peat moss (which has a pH below 5.0) and work it well into the soil; otherwise the peat moss can form a crust that is almost impenetrable to water. Peat moss also adds organic matter, which helps to retain moisture.

2 Alternatively, to make the soil more acidic, add garden sulfur or aluminum sulfate to the soil.

Yellow flag iris (I. pseudacorus) is a species that blossoms in late spring. It grows in conditions similar to those of Japanese iris, but can even tolerate standing water.

BEARDED IRIS
Iris x *germanica*

Zones: 3–10

Bloom Time: Early summer

Light: Full sun

Height: 8–36 in.

Interest: Brilliant blooms; many sweetly fragrant

Bearded irises provide flamboyance to any garden because they come in dwarf, intermediate, and tall sizes. The brilliant colors of the blossoms are often unique to the world of flowers and were created by complicated hybridization. Some people consider bearded irises untidy looking after the flowers fade. Instead, they prefer to grow these delicious beauties in an area by themselves, or in a location where the sword-like leaves will be hidden by neighboring plants.

HOW TO GROW
Bearded irises prefer full sun, though in warmer regions they like some light shade. Proper planting is very important (see sidebar). Grow these beauties in loose, fertile soil that has been amended with organic matter.

Iris borer is a major pest that tunnels into the thick rhizome. If you see spots like water streaks on leaves, feel the rhizome tops for soft spots; dig up any suspicious rhizomes to look for (and destroy) white borers inside. To reduce susceptibility, space plants 12 to 18 inches apart for best air circulation, and do not mulch.

WHERE TO GROW

Bearded irises are available in tall (the most common), intermediate, and dwarf forms. Plant tall forms in the middle or back of perennial borders or in mass plantings. Intermediate types look charming toward the front of the border. Dwarf forms bloom slightly earlier than tall bearded varieties and make nice additions to rock and specialty gardens and near the front of the border.

Top Choices

- *I.* 'Amber Ambush' is a dwarf (8 to 14 inches) whose apricot flowers are tinged with magenta.

- *I.* 'Beverly Sills' grows to 36 inches tall with ruffled, light pink flowers.

- *I.* 'Blue Staccato' has white petals edged with dark blue on 40-inch stems.

- *I.* 'Candy Apple' is a bright burgundy dwarf that grows only 8 to 14 inches tall.

- *I.* 'Edith Wolford' is a charming ruffled bicolor with lemon yellow standards and violet falls (lower petals).

- *I.* 'Vanity' has a right to be vain, with its beautiful, fragrant, clear pink flowers.

PLANTING RHIZOMES

Plant iris rhizomes in well-drained soil in late summer.

1 Dig a hole large enough to accommodate all roots; form a ridge of soil in the bottom.

2 Spread roots out over the ridge. Add more soil as needed until rhizomes sit horizontal to the soil level. Cover with ½ inch of soil.

3 Divide the roots every three to four years to keep plants vigorous.

CHOOSE THE PICK OF THE CROP

With so many bearded iris varieties available and new ones being developed, it is difficult to pick among them. Find a grower whose fields you can roam when the plants are in full bloom and choose your favorites for later shipment. If you shop from catalogs, look for award-winning varieties; then you know that other gardeners like them, too—not just the hybridizer.

SIBERIAN IRIS
Iris sibirica

Zones: 3–8

Bloom Time: Early summer

Light: Full sun to light shade

Height: 24–36 in.

Interest: Beautiful flowers of various colors; handsome green foliage

Siberian iris ranks among the world's most-loved garden plants for its abundant, attractive flowers and handsome, swordlike foliage that remains attractive throughout the growing season. Through careful breeding, hybridizers have produced a host of flower colors in many shades of blue, purple, white, bicolors, and even yellow. They have also doubled the size of the flowers of some varieties. The plants are impervious to pests and diseases, requiring almost no care. Barring unforeseen catastrophes, they'll grace your garden forever.

HOW TO GROW
Siberian iris needs full sun or light shade. Plant in any good garden soil, either moist or dry. In most soils you won't need to water much—the roots reach down deeply for moisture. However, the plants do require watering in

sandy soils. Once established, Siberian irises never need dividing, but to increase the number of plants (or reduce the size of large clumps), carefully dig them up in late summer, divide the crowns (this may require a large, sharp knife), and replant. Siberian iris grows vigorously in late summer and early fall; dividing in late summer allows divisions to reestablish themselves before winter. The only care required is deadheading and cutting down the foliage after two or three killing frosts in late fall.

WHERE TO GROW

Grow Siberian irises in borders by themselves, in mixed borders, island beds, containers, and in the cutting garden. They are wonderful anywhere in your garden.

Top Choices

- *I.* 'Butter and Sugar' grows 28 inches tall and has white standards (upright petals) and unique yellow falls (lower petals). This hybrid created a sensation when it was introduced, as it was the first really yellow variety.

- *I.* 'Fourfold White' has very large, pure white flowers (each with a prominent gold spot at the base) on 30-inch stems.

- *I.* 'Super Ego' lives up to its name with its pale blue standards and falls of the same hue on 32-inch plants. The showy blooms are heavily shaded and veined with a deeper blue.

Garden Companions

It is impossible to plant Siberian iris with the "wrong" plant—so plant it wherever you want its attractive and colorful presence in your garden. Some of its especially good companions include:

- BALLOON FLOWER
- ORIENTAL POPPIES
- PEACHLEAF BELLFLOWER
- PEONIES
- PERENNIAL GERANIUMS
- SUNDROPS
- WILD INDIGO
- YARROWS

'Butter and Sugar', like other Siberian irises, provides you with beautiful flowers year after year with little effort.

PERENNIAL SWEET PEA
Lathyrus latifolius

Zones: 4–9

Bloom Time: All summer to early fall

Light: Full sun

Height: To 10 ft.

Interest: Freely flowering vine

The perennial sweet pea, also called everlasting pea, is an easy-to-grow vine with white, pale pink, or rose red flowers. Unlike the fussy annual sweet pea, it requires little attention. In fact, it's so versatile and so maintenance-free it's often planted along highways as a colorful, attractive ground cover. Perennial sweet pea lacks only one element of horticultural perfection: the incredible fragrance of its annual counterpart.

HOW TO GROW

Perennial sweet pea thrives in a wide range of growing conditions and is not fussy about soil—just avoid waterlogged sites. It requires almost no maintenance; simply remove seedpods to keep the vines blooming prolifically through summer. It's best to leave the plants undisturbed once planted since the roots grow deeply (as they do for many members of the pea or legume family). Perennial sweet pea thrives in full sun but prefers cool, moist soil for the most vigorous growth. Add a 2-inch layer of mulch, such as leaf compost, around the root area after planting to keep soil cool. Renew mulch in spring if necessary. Though the plants produce pods filled with seeds like garden peas, be sure to instruct children that the seeds of perennial sweet pea are not to be eaten.

WHERE TO GROW

This colorful vine can provide a vertical accent when grown on a trellis in a mixed border. A more horizontal look is attained by allowing plants to scramble along a fence. Planted near shrubs, perennial sweet pea can climb through branches, adding sprinklings of color to bushes whose flowering time has passed. As a ground cover, plants sprawl over the soil while brightening the view. The flowers make charming little bouquets, so plant lots along the fence around your vegetable garden.

Top Choices

- *L.* 'Rose Pearl' has pink flowers touched with white.

- *L.* 'Splendens' has blossoms of dark reddish purple.

- *L.* 'White Pearl' is named for its pearl-like white flowers.

GROWING VINES IN A BORDER

Use twining vines such as the perennial sweet pea, clematis, and some honeysuckles to add vertical dimension to a border. Avoid heavy or very vigorous growers such as wisteria or trumpet vine.

❶ Purchase or build an 8- to 10-foot-tall pyramid structure of rot-resistant material such as Eastern red cedar or pressure-treated wood. Anchor well, attaching the support legs to rot-resistant stakes driven at least 3 feet into the ground. Fasten with galvanized wire or stainless-steel pipe clamps.

❷ Plant a vine or two at the base and guide the shoots up the tower legs. Tie plants loosely to legs to help them get a good start.

❸ Remove spent blossoms and keep well watered; avoid overwatering. Vines such as clematis resent wet feet and collapse if the soil remains waterlogged.

ENGLISH LAVENDER
Lavandula angustifolia

Zones: 5–10

Bloom Time: Mid-summer

Light: Full sun

Height: 12–36 in.

Interest: Wonderfully fragrant flowers; attractive, compact plants with silvery gray foliage

The fragrance of lavender has enjoyed a long history as a favored ingredient in soaps and perfumes. The lovely plants are a welcome addition to any garden for their beauty and fragrance. English lavender is a compact plant that usually grows to about 24 inches tall with very attractive silvery gray evergreen foliage. Flowers bloom on 12-inch stems that are ideal for cutting. The uses of lavender flowers are legendary, including dried arrangements, perfume, potpourri, wreaths, sachets, herb pillows, teas, and flavoring in oils and vinegars.

HOW TO GROW

Lavender must be grown in full sun and well-drained soil that is slightly acidic to slightly alkaline. Winter wetness sitting around the crowns of plants is one of the main reasons it fails to thrive. It is also short-lived in the humid South. Shear the plants heavily in spring as soon as new growth starts to appear. Plants may be propagated from seeds, but named varieties must be reproduced from stem cuttings.

WHERE TO GROW

Lavender may be featured in an herb garden, toward the front of a mixed border, or on the south side of a house as a unique foundation planting. It is superb when planted with old-fashioned roses and unrivaled when used as a low hedge. It is also an excellent container plant for a sunny patio or deck. Plant lots for your use; otherwise you may find yourself tempted to strip the fragrant blossoms from the plants in your flower garden.

Top Choices

- *L.* 'Hidcote' has a compact form with very dark violet-blue blossoms on tidy, 20-inch plants.

- *L.* 'Munstead Dwarf' is similar to the above except the flowers are a deep shade of heliotrope purple and the plants only grow to 12 inches tall.

- *L.* 'Rosea' is a pink-flowered selection on 15-inch plants. 'Jean Davis' and 'Loddon Pink' are almost identical.

- *L.* x *intermedia* 'Grosso' is a superb hybrid with deep violet-blue flowers and long, straight stems on 24-inch plants. Especially fragrant, it is widely grown for oil and for drying.

DRYING LAVENDER

Dried lavender adds a blue note, not to mention a sweet, heady scent, to potpourri and floral arrangements. To dry lavender:

1 Clip off the stems just above the foliage as soon as the flowers are fully open and at their most pungent. If you prefer the look of unopened buds, which hold up much better in potpourri and arrangements, clip stems when buds are fully formed but before any have opened.

2 Tie together in bundles of thirty to forty stems.

3 Hang the bundles upside down in a dry, well-ventilated place. Leave them to dry for three to four weeks.

4 Use in dried arrangements or wreaths. Strip off the individual flowers for other purposes such as sachets, potpourris, and teas.

5 You can also stand dried lavender in a dry vase and do nothing else. The softly scented flower stalks will last the winter through.

SHASTA DAISY
Leucanthemum x *superbum*

Zones: 4–9

Bloom Time: Summer

Light: Full sun

Height: 12–36 in.

Interest: Large white daisies; attractive dark green foliage

For people who love white daisies, Shastas reign supreme. Previously known as *Chrysanthemum* x *superbum,* these hybrids were first created by the American plantsman Luther Burbank, and have become a mainstay of the perennial border. Shastas are tidy, well-behaved plants that require only a little attention to put on a delightful show of flowers for most of summer. The basal foliage remains evergreen during winter, adding a touch of rich dark green to the otherwise brown border. Since they bloom all summer and they last a long time in water, Shastas make superb cut flowers.

HOW TO GROW

This low-maintenance perennial performs best in rich, well-drained soil with liberal applications of organic matter. Full sun and regular watering during drought conditions are essential. Shasta daisies put on their best show if they are fertilized with a low-nitrogen plant food in early spring. Deadhead to keep the plants looking neat. Shasta daisies produce strong stems and do not need staking. Maintain plant vigor by dividing the crowns every two to three years. You can also start them from seeds that come remarkably true to variety.

WHERE TO GROW

Some say Shasta daisies belong in every sunny, well-drained perennial or mixed border. Like most white-flowered plants, they can be used to separate colors that clash. Since there are tall (36 inches) and short (12 inches) varieties, they can be used in the middle of a border or at the front. Shastas make excellent container plants for a patio or deck.

Top Choices

- *L.* 'Alaska' is very hardy and has 2-inch, single flowers on 2- to 2½-foot stems.

- *L.* 'Becky' grows 3 to 4 feet tall and flowers late with 4-inch, single blossoms.

- *L.* 'Little Miss Muffet' grows to a height of 12 inches with 2- to 3-inch, semidouble blooms.

- *L.* 'Marconi' is 24 to 36 inches with frilly, 3- to 4-inch, fully double blooms.

- *L.* 'Polaris' is 24 to 36 inches tall with 4- to 5-inch, single blooms.

SHASTA DAISIES FOR BOUQUETS

All Shasta daisies have well-formed, attractive flowers. Several varieties also have long, sturdy stems and large blooms, making them perfect for fresh summer bouquets. They include:

- 'Aglaya'—white, double flower
- 'Cobham Gold'—pale yellow with a darker center
- 'Polar Sun'—fringed white petals
- 'Silver Princess'—white, semi-double blossoms
- 'Thomas Killen'—large, white, single flowers

CONTROLLING PESKY BUGS

Japanese beetles are somewhat fond of Shasta daisies. One of the surest ways to get rid of these pests is to pick them off early in the morning while the beetles are groggy (they do have a very active social life). Wear rubber gloves if you find their touch distasteful. To drown the captured beetles, drop them into a jar filled with water and a shot of dishwashing detergent.

GAY-FEATHER
Liatris spicata

Zones: 3–8

Bloom Time: Mid- to late summer

Light: Full sun

Height: 36–48 in.

Interest: Tall, rosy purple (or white) vertical spikes, attractive to bees and butterflies

Native to North America, liatris (it's more commonly known by its Latin name) is a must for the border. It provides a colorful, vertical accent, makes a superb cut flower (florists use it liberally), and is useful in dried arrangements. Liatris blends in well with perennials of many other shades; in fact it's hard to find a color it resents being next to. It's also a "no-brainer," requiring virtually no maintenance and no trouble whatsoever to keep it flourishing! Liatris attracts butterflies and bees to its blossoms and goldfinches to its seedpods in fall.

HOW TO GROW
Although tolerant of a wide variety of soil types, liatris thrives best in good garden soil that stays evenly moist and is well supplied with nutrients. Shoots are somewhat slow to appear in spring, so mark locations well and

take care not to damage the tuberous roots when you're scratching around nearby. In rich soil or partial shade, the spikes grow taller and may require staking; be careful to avoid piercing the roots when setting stakes. Remove the entire spike to the top of the foliage after all the flowers have gone by—they open from the top downward. Liatris are all grown from seeds and are relatively inexpensive to purchase as dormant roots at garden centers.

WHERE TO GROW

Liatris is ideal for the mixed border, providing a strong architectural element. Space permitting, it looks best planted in masses. Place in the middle or the front of a mixed planting so that you can enjoy it to the maximum, but also to get a close look at butterflies that swarm to feast on its nectar.

Top Choices

- *L.* 'Floristan Violet' has large spikes of beautifully deep rose-violet flowers on 36-inch-tall plants.

- *L.* 'Floristan White', a pure white German selection produced for the cut-flower trade, is equally at home in American gardens.

- *L.* 'Kobold' is a sturdy dwarf form (24 to 30 inches) with reddish lilac blossoms from July to September. It never needs staking.

- *L. ligulistylis* is totally irresistible to butterflies in early fall, especially monarchs. It grows to 60 inches tall, usually requiring staking with slender bamboo canes.

STAKING PLANTS WITH TALL SPIKES

Staking tall plants with strongly upright spikes of flowers is best done with a very thin bamboo cane or a ¼-inch metal rod. Stake each flower spike as it reaches close to its mature height, but before the individual flowers open.

1 Push a support at least 12 inches into the ground and close to each flower spike—making sure you don't damage the fleshy roots of plants such as liatris. The stake should be just slightly shorter than the mature height of the spike.

2 Carefully arrange the leaves and flower buds so that the stem is next to the stake. Tie loosely with green string or a soft, green plastic tie. Stakes will be invisible when the spike is fully open if this is done carefully.

DIVIDE TO
REJUVENATE

Most perennials bloom less vigorously after a few years unless divided. Cut the existing clump into two or four pieces with a sharp spade. Discard central portions that are no longer vigorous. Enrich the soil before replanting one or two of the divisions. Give the other pieces away, or move them to another spot.

HOLLYHOCK MALLOW
Malva alcea var. *fastigiata*

Zones: 4–9

Bloom Time: Summer

Light: Full to part sun

Height: 36–48 in.

Interest: Masses of pink blossoms like miniature hollyhocks

Hollyhock mallow is an easy-to-grow perennial that blooms with 2-inch clear pink flowers over a very long period during the summer. The flowers appear on bushy plants that grow 3 to 4 feet tall and almost as wide—so they are a significant presence in a border. Best of all, mallow is not too fussy. It never needs staking in full sun, is tolerant of dry soil conditions, and it flowers profusely.

HOW TO GROW

Hollyhock mallow fares well in ordinary garden soil. Blooming slows only if the soil is allowed to get too dry during hot, rainless spells. Plants become floppy in shade, so stake with brushwood (see page 29) in partial shade before they come into bloom. Hollyhock mallow self-sows freely; remove unwanted seedlings as soon as they appear, or remove seedpods before they drop their seeds. This can be a tedious task, but it's worth the effort.

WHERE TO GROW

This delightful plant is an ideal addition to the mixed border, where its size and form give it the appearance of a compact shrub. It is also useful in foundation plantings where winter interest is not a factor. It can be planted in the middle of a border or toward the center of an island bed that features other medium-sized plants. It looks especially good with other brushy perennials. Mallow also makes a great container plant since it flowers for such a long time. On a patio or deck, the faded blossoms can easily be removed to promote even more flowers.

Top Choices

- *M. moschata*, musk mallow, is available in pink or white ('Alba'). It also seeds freely; it is very much at home in a cottage garden. Zones 3 to 8.

- *M. sylvestris* 'Primley Blue' is very easy to grow. It has blue flowers striped with a deeper tone of the same.

- *M. sylvestris* 'Zebrina' produces dramatic flowers that are pale lilac-pink, striped with dark purplish red. It is a short-lived perennial or biennial, so allow some seeds to fall each year. Zones 3 to 9.

HELP PLANTS KEEP THEIR COOL

Many perennials, such as hollyhock mallow and Frikart's aster, are most vigorous and bloom best when their roots are kept moist and cool. To keep your perennials comfortable and in peak bloom:

- Before planting, mix plenty of organic matter into the soil to a depth of about 12 inches.

- Install a soaker hose throughout the garden to deliver moisture to the plants most efficiently.

- Add a layer of organic mulch around plants to retard evaporation and shield soil from direct sunlight. Keep mulch 2 inches from plant crowns.

RELOCATING SEEDLINGS

After you plant one mallow, you will soon have seedlings all over the garden. If you plan on relocating a mallow seedling, you will need to do so while it is very small—before the plant grows a long taproot.

The day before transplanting, water the seedling well to help limit the shock and to loosen the soil. Replant the seedling in a hole deep enough so the plant is at the same or a slightly deeper level than it was growing previously.

BEE BALM

Monarda didyma

Zones: 4–8

Bloom Time: Mid- to late summer

Light: Full sun to part shade

Height: 30–42 in.

Interest: Unique blooms in a range of colors; spicily fragrant foliage; attractive to butterflies and hummingbirds

Bee balm is an invaluable plant for the perennial border. Its flowers come in a variety of shades and sit atop spicily scented foliage. Older varieties suffer from powdery mildew, but if plants are grown at the back of the border where the leaves are less obvious, this is not a problem worth concern. The leaves of this member of the mint family make a fine tea.

HOW TO GROW

Bee balm will grow in almost any soil, but it thrives best in those that are evenly moist. Drying out causes stress, which increases mildew; water well during hot, dry spells. Don't cut the stems back until spring, as the dead spikes are interesting in winter, especially against a snowscape; the foliage and seed heads retain their pungency even in a desiccated state. Bee balm spreads by underground runners and can be invasive; if it threatens to engulf your garden, just chop off edges of the clumps and transplant them, give them away, or compost them. Allow them to dry out completely before composting. Otherwise they'll grow and run rampant in the compost heap!

WHERE TO GROW

Plant bee balm at the back of the perennial border or toward the center of an island bed. It also looks great in a wild garden or in a meadow where the free-spreading plants can romp gleefully. Since hummingbirds love the flowers, plant bee balm near your kitchen window so you can enjoy these flashing rainbows of color up close.

Top Choices

- M. 'Gardenview Scarlet' has scarlet red, 3-inch flowers and resists mildew.

- M. 'Marshall's Delight', a pink-flowered Canadian that is mildew-resistant, is more compact than older pink varieties.

- M. 'Raspberry Wine', true to its name, has raspberry red flowers above attractive dark bracts.

- M. 'Snow White' is a pure white variety that looks best planted among the other shades of bee balm.

- M. fistulosa, wild bergamot, with its light lavender to pink flowers, is more tolerant of dry conditions and poor soil than the M. didyma hybrids.

MAKING HERBAL TEAS

Since the Boston Tea Party, various alternatives to black tea have been used as a refreshing drink and as remedies for various ailments. Today, their popularity has grown as health-conscious individuals choose to avoid the caffeine in black tea. Plants such as bee balm, chamomile, lemon verbena, and many mints make appealing teas.

1 For each cup of water, mix 1 tablespoon fresh leaves with 1 tablespoon dried leaves (of the same plant or another).

2 In true English fashion, "warm the pot" by rinsing it with boiling water. Put the leaves in the warmed teapot. (Some say tea is best when brewed in and sipped from bone china.)

3 Pour boiling (not lukewarm) water over the leaves and allow to steep for 5 or more minutes. Since herb teas don't color the water, taste it to be sure it has steeped long enough.

4 Strain tea and add honey, sugar, a sprig of mint, a slice of lemon, or sweetener (if you really must).

CATMINT
Nepeta x *faassenii*

Zones: 3–8

Bloom Time: Summer

Light: Full sun to light shade

Height: 18–24 in.

Interest: Long-lasting, tall spikes of lavender-blue; pungent gray foliage

Catmint is a delightful plant with tall, wispy spikes of lavender-blue flowers over grayish green foliage that releases a pungent aroma when brushed. *N.* x *faassenii* is the most commonly grown variety. Catmint is invaluable for blending with soft colors and providing a backdrop for strong ones. It is easy to grow in most conditions except the high heat and humidity of the Deep South.

HOW TO GROW
Catmint is not terribly fussy about soil; it tolerates dry conditions better than most perennials. The taller forms may need staking, though their informal habit is appreciated by some. If you are the tidy type, place brushwood staking (see page 29) by the plants before they fall over. Cutting back the plants after the main flush of

flowers has passed will ensure a strong second flush later in summer.

WHERE TO GROW

This plant belongs in every perennial border, shrub border, and rose garden, where it will add color and interest long after its companions have stopped blooming. There are very few colors that it doesn't look good planted alongside, but it is especially appealing near plants with pale yellow flowers.

Top Choices

- N. 'Blue Wonder' has abundant blue-violet flowers on compact plants. Zones 4 to 7.

- N. 'Dropmore' has rich, deep blue blossoms on well-branched plants. Zones 4 to 7.

- N. 'Six Hills Giant' grows to 36 inches tall with masses of lavender-blue flowers on informal, floppy stems. It is more tolerant of humid summers than other catmints. Zones 4 to 8.

- N. *sibirica,* Siberian catmint, 'Blue Beauty' has deep blue flower spikes that last for several weeks; it grows 24 to 36 inches tall.

PINNING A RUNNER

Although usually grown from seeds, catmint can be propagated by carefully pinning a runner to the ground. To try this method of propagation:

1 Use a hairpin-shaped wire, a small rock, or a small pile of soil to pin the runner to the ground in the desired location.

2 Water regularly and, after a few weeks, remove the pin or rock. Check to see if roots have formed where the runner contacts the ground.

3 If rooted, snip the runner so you can dig up the new plant. Replant it where desired, shading it for the first couple of days to minimize transplant shock.

FRAGRANCE IN THE GARDEN

While it's common to think of flowers in bloom when you think of a fragrant garden, you can add even more aroma by using plants with fragrant flowers and those with aromatic foliage.

For example, try planting catmint and lavender along the walkways of your rose garden for a delightful blend of scents and a visually enticing mix of floral colors and textures.

SUNDROPS
Oenothera fruticosa

Zones: 4–9

Bloom Time: Early to midsummer

Light: Full sun

Height: 18–24 in.

Interest: Golden yellow blooms that contrast wonderfully with the reddish flower buds

Sundrops lives up to its name, lending the garden some of the brightest shades of yellow possible. This native of eastern North America turns out an abundance of reddish to deep red buds that open into sunny, upward-facing blossoms. The result is a color combination no warm-toned garden should be without.

HOW TO GROW

Sundrops grows easily in ordinary garden soil; it tolerates dry conditions and poor soil low in nutrients. Planting in shade as well as overfertilizing result in few flowers and excess leaves. Sundrops spreads quickly by underground runners. Its shallow roots make the plants easy to remove if they pop up where unwanted.

WHERE TO GROW

Plant sundrops toward the front of a mixed border or in a rock garden, or use it under open shrubs as a vibrant ground cover. It looks especially attractive when planted next to reddish purple flowers or any shade of blue, and it positively shines when planted in front of plants with blue, copper, bronze, or reddish purple foliage (see "Garden Companions"at right).

Top Choices

- O. 'Fireworks' has deep red, 18-inch-tall stems topped with red buds that open to bright yellow flowers in early summer.

- O. 'Highlight' has large, very bright yellow flowers that emit a light fragrance. The blossoms are arranged in clusters atop 15-inch stems.

- O. 'Solstice' (also called 'Summer Solstice'), with deep red buds and stems, is one of the best selections. It offers repeat blooms in late summer.

- O. 'Yellow River' has 18-inch-tall, medium green buds and stems with large, vivid yellow flowers.

- O. *speciosa* 'Rosea' bears large, pale pink blossoms at the top of 15-inch-tall plants. Zones 5 to 9.

Garden Companions

The sunshine yellow flowers of sundrops contrast beautifully with the darker tones of blue and purple that the following plants provide:

- BLUE OAT GRASS
- BLUESTAR
- CATMINT
- 'HUSKER RED' BEARD-TONGUE
- PERENNIAL GERANIUMS
- PURPLE SMOKEBUSH
- SIBERIAN IRISES
- WILD INDIGO

THE GROUND COVER
ALTERNATIVE

Of all the plants—trees, shrubs, perennials, and annuals—you may plant in your yard, it is the lawn that usually demands the most water and the most care. Increasingly, gardeners in locales susceptible to dry weather are turning to the ground cover as a colorful, drought-tolerant alternative to grass. Once established, ground covers require very little maintenance while adding a splash of color to a traditional landscape.

PEONY

Paeonia

Zones: 3–8

Bloom Time: Late spring

Light: Full sun

Height: 36 in.

Interest: Very large, sometimes fragrant blossoms with single or double flowers; dark green, shrublike foliage with good fall color

When professional plantsmen talk about essential plants for the garden, peonies rank near the top of the list. In part, their reputation comes from their dominant presence, in or out of flower. The foliage is a rich dark green that sets off the blossoms perfectly and, after the flowers have gone, gives the plants the demeanor of small shrubs. Peony blossoms come in variations of two forms: double and single. Double-flowered varieties bear large, dramatic flowers packed with showy petals. Single-flowered varieties are less bold, with silky petals and graceful elegance. Most single-flowered peonies have strong, upright stems and, unlike double-flowered forms, rarely require staking. Japanese peonies are single-flowered varieties that have an outer row of petals around an attractive cluster of petal-like stamens. With proper care, peonies live longer than most other plants.

HOW TO GROW

Peonies require rich soil with good drainage and lots of organic matter to hold moisture. Feed peonies in early spring and late fall with a low-nitrogen fertilizer. Double-flowered peonies tend to flop over and need to be staked. Place four to six sturdy 4-foot bamboo canes around each young plant. As the plant grows, lace soft string or green garden tape around the stakes. Make sure one string goes diagonally across the center of the plant to give the individual stems more support.

WHERE TO GROW

Because peonies figure so prominently in a border, they should be set in place first, as accent points, with the rest of the design developed to complement them. As foundation plantings or low hedges, they're magnificent on their own and they make truly superb cut flowers. In warm areas where winters are mild, it is best to grow early-flowering varieties that finish growing before the heat of the summer.

Top Choices

- *P.* 'Festiva Maxima' has large, fragrant, double flowers; its pure white petals are accented with a few crimson streaks.

- *P.* 'Kansas' produces bright watermelon red, double blooms on 36-inch plants.

- *P.* 'Krinkled White' has pure white, single blooms with crinkled petals surrounding a mound of bright golden yellow stamens.

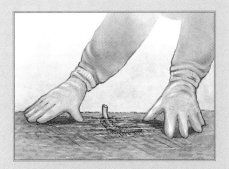

PLANTING PEONIES

Peonies should be planted in fall from dormant roots. Planting in spring is possible, but only when they are grown in a biodegradable container that can be completely buried. Take care to place the crown of the plant two inches deep; if you don't, flowers will be few or nonexistent.

1 Dig a hole twice as large as the size of the root mass. Work well-rotted manure or leaf compost into the bottom of the hole.

2 In the center of the hole, make a slight dome on which to place the roots. Plant the dormant buds two inches below the surface of the soil. This is a critical measurement.

3 Fill and firm the soil, making sure to compress it beside the roots. Caution: Never press down on the crown, as the buds may snap off.

ORIENTAL POPPY
Papaver orientale

Zones: 2–7

Bloom Time: Early summer

Light: Full sun

Height: 24–36 in.

Interest: Large, showy flowers in delicate to brilliant shades; interesting seedpods after petals have fallen

For a few weeks each summer, Oriental poppies provide one of the most spectacular shows in the perennial garden. They produce a barrage of 4- to 6-inch blossoms in clear shades of pink, salmon, orange, red, or white, often with black markings at the centers. For sheer drama, a bed of poppies is a sight that's hard to beat. Poppy foliage appears very early in the year with large, rich green leaves that are rough to the touch. If planted in well-prepared soil, poppies become very long-lived plants that perform indefinitely without much care.

HOW TO GROW
Oriental poppies prefer deeply dug, rich garden soil that their fleshy roots can penetrate easily. They tolerate dry soils, but not poor drainage. Give careful thought to where you want them—if they're moved later, new plants

will appear from pieces of root left behind. Poppies prefer full sun. Add organic matter and a low-nitrogen fertilizer next to the crowns in late winter. Cut back the foliage or divide after plants go dormant.

WHERE TO GROW

Oriental poppies look most dramatic when interplanted among colorful annuals and late- blooming perennials. These plants hide the yellow foliage as the poppies go dormant later in summer. Alongside poppies, plant a few irises or some pastel peonies to add softness beside the brilliant poppy flowers.

Top Choices

- *P.* 'Allegro' is scarlet with dramatic black spots in its center.

- *P.* 'Helen Elizabeth' has delightfully ruffled, pale pink flowers. It blooms earlier than most varieties.

- *P.* 'Oriental' is brilliant orange-red with prominent black basal spots, and is one of the strongest, most vigorous growers.

- *P.* 'Pinnacle' is perhaps one of the most beautiful, with ruffled and crinkled white flowers that are banded with apricot-pink on the edges.

- *P.* 'Türkenlouis' is very exotic looking with frilly-edged, bright red blossoms and black blotches in the center.

- *P.* 'Victoria Dreyfuss' has dark salmon, 7-inch blossoms that are edged with silvery white.

POPPIES IN BOUQUETS

A classic late-spring or early summer bouquet consists of a few stalks of Siberian iris such as 'Butter and Sugar' or 'Fourfold White'; one or two peony blossoms such as 'Festiva Maxima'; and, to round things out, a few Oriental poppies such as 'Helen Elizabeth' and 'Pinnacle'.

To keep Oriental poppies in arrangements looking perky and fresh for the longest possible time, be sure to flame the ends of the stem after cutting (see page 105).

PLANTING ORIENTAL POPPIES

Fall is the best time of year to plant Oriental poppies. For them to thrive, it is very important to plant them more deeply than is the norm for other perennials. Be sure to plant the crown (the area where the foliage and roots meet) three inches below the soil surface—no more, no less.

BEARD-TONGUE
Penstemon barbatus

Zones: 3–9

Bloom Time: Early summer

Light: Full sun

Height: 18–36 in.

Interest: Masses of tube-shaped flowers; recurrent bloom until frost

Though native to the Southwest and Mexico, beard-tongue is perfectly hardy in the North and thrives in the heat and humidity of the Deep South. The small flowers, arranged along the stems (similar to foxglove), appear in shades of lavender, pink, red, purple, and white. Even in the darker colors, the effect is airy, and the plant adds a delicate presence to the late-June border among more flamboyant neighbors.

HOW TO GROW

Beard-tongue requires ordinary but well-drained garden soil. It needs full sun in northern gardens, but prefers partial shade in the Southeast. Be certain to keep mulches away from the crown, as the plant will rot quickly if smothered. Remove dead flower spikes to encourage repeat blooming.

WHERE TO GROW

Place beard-tongue anywhere toward the front of a mixed border where you want a touch of subtlety. Shorter-growing varieties are ideal for the rock garden. All sizes are stunning in cut flower arrangements.

Top Choices

- *P.* 'Bashful' has orange-red blossoms on 12- to 14-inch stems.

- *P.* 'Prairie Dusk' is a dusky purplish red with 18- to 24-inch stems.

- *P.* 'Rose Elf' is a vigorous variety with coral pink blooms on 18- to 22-inch spikes.

- *P.* 'Ruby' is an aptly named deep red selection on 18-to 24-inch stems.

- *P.* 'Twilight' is a seed strain with a delightful mix of colors and heights.

- *P. digitalis* 'Husker Red' is one of the best perennial introductions of recent years. Its pure white flowers on 36-inch spikes wave above bronzy red foliage.

Garden Companions

Beard-tongue is an excellent plant to use as a filler between bold plants. It also complements large groups of softer-colored flowers. Try planting with any of these for starters:

- ARTEMESIA 'SILVER MOUND'
- COLUMBINES
- FRIKART'S ASTER
- ORIENTAL POPPIES
- PERENNIAL GERANIUMS
- THREADLEAF COREOPSIS

AVOIDING CROWN ROT

Beard-tongue can be susceptible to crown rot. Obvious signs of the disease are fan-shaped white fungal threads (mycelia) at the base of the stem; these may spread over the surrounding ground in wet weather. To help avoid this disease, add organic matter such as peat moss or compost to the soil when plant ing and keep mulch two inches away from plant crowns.

RUSSIAN SAGE

Perovskia atriplicifolia

Zones: 5–9

Bloom Time: Mid- to late summer

Light: Full sun

Height: 36–60 in.

Interest: An elegant, pungently fragrant, shrubby perennial with lavender blossoms and gray foliage

Ignore the common name: Russian sage is not Russian at all, nor is it a sage (although it has a sagelike odor and belongs to the same family). It is, however, a superb plant whose silvery gray foliage, clouds of lavender blossoms, and enticing fragrance should win it a place in every sunny garden. It makes an excellent cut flower if cut when the flowers are young; however, the pungency may be somewhat overpowering in small, poorly ventilated rooms.

HOW TO GROW

Grow Russian sage in any well-drained garden soil; the richer the soil, the more vigorously the plant will grow. Like many large plants, this one looks its best and performs best when it has room to spread out. It is impervious to pests and requires no maintenance except an annual pruning to 6 to 8 inches in late winter. In crowded situations it may require staking; this can be avoided by pinching out the growing tips of the main shoots in mid-June (three weeks earlier in the South).

WHERE TO GROW

This plant's graceful presence makes it welcome anywhere in the garden. Give Russian sage a place of honor in the mixed border or the rose garden, or use it to enliven ho-hum foundation plantings. To enjoy Russian sage's fragrance and airy beauty all the more, be sure to plant some in a container on a patio, terrace, or deck.

Top Choices

- *P.* 'Blue Haze' has flowers and leaves of pale blue.

- *P.* 'Blue Spire' is identical in color to the species but has lacier foliage.

- *P.* 'Filagran' has an upright habit and blue flowers on 36-inch-tall stems.

- *P.* 'Longin' is slightly more erect than the species with flowers of a similar color.

- *P.* 'Superba' has violet-blue blossoms and is considered one of the finest Russian sage selections.

Garden Companions

All roses, but especially shrub roses, are wonderful companions for Russian sage. Consider these selections as well:

- BLUEBEARDS
- CULVER'S ROOT
- DAYLILIES
- FEATHER GRASS
- GARDEN PHLOX
- HELENIUMS
- HOLLYHOCK MALLOW
- PERENNIAL GERANIUMS
- PURPLE SAGE
- QUEEN-OF-THE-PRAIRIE

WATER TRANSFORMS

The simple addition of water to a garden, in the form of a pond or fountain, can have a subtle yet transforming effect, but be careful not to get carried away with this landscaping element. It shouldn't dominate the garden. After planting your garden, assess the space you have left. In a small area, try a birdbath or an elegant fountain, scaled appropriately for the space. For a larger area, a modest pool might be a very satisfying element to add.

GARDEN PHLOX

Phlox paniculata

Zones: 4–8

Bloom Time: Late summer

Light: Full sun

Height: 30–48 in.

Interest: Beautiful clusters of perky, fragrant flowers in many shades

Garden phlox has been a part of refined perennial gardens for decades. Today's varieties blend nostalgia and sophistication with a vigorous, no-nonsense nature that makes them beautiful and easy to grow. Garden phlox brightens up the late-summer border at a time when most perennials are past their peak. It comes in many colors, including bright lavender, pink, purple, red, and white. Some varieties have a central eye of a contrasting color. Most have a delightful sweet perfume. All are excellent cut flowers and may be cut as soon as at least a third of the blossoms have opened.

HOW TO GROW

Garden phlox requires well-drained soil that doesn't dry out, so be liberal with organic matter. Water thoroughly during dry spells using soaker hoses; avoid overhead sprinklers, which encourage the spread of mildew. Feed the plants in early spring and late fall with a low-nitrogen fertilizer; avoid overcrowding by removing half the new shoots as they appear. If mildew is a problem in your area, select varieties that are mildew-resistant. In windy locations, stake plants with brushwood (see page 29) when they're about a foot high. Deadhead to prolong the blooming period.

WHERE TO GROW

Garden phlox is a classic plant for the middle of the border. Surround it with contrasting colors but take care not to crowd it; garden phlox needs plenty of ventilation. In front, plant peonies; the rich foliage will showcase phlox's flowers but hide any foliage afflicted with powdery mildew. Be sure to plant enough phlox for cutting. It is a sweet-smelling addition to late-summer garden bouquets.

Top Choices

- *P.* 'Bright Eyes' has alluring blush pink blossoms dotted with a crimson eye.

- *P.* 'David' is mildew-resistant. Pure white flowers bloom on plants 40 inches tall. It is the best white variety.

- *P.* 'Eva Cullum' features clear pink blossoms with a dark red eye on plants that grow 30 to 36 inches tall.

- *P.* 'Franz Schubert' is a recent introduction. Its lilac bloom has a star-shaped eye. Plants grow 36 to 40 inches tall.

- *P.* 'Starfire' is the best red variety. The blossoms are cherry red atop 36-inch stems.

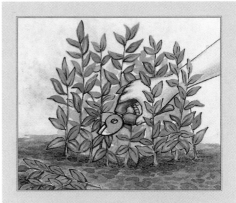

THINNING TO REDUCE POWDERY MILDEW

Powdery mildew appears as a white dust on the upper surfaces of leaves of plants such as phlox, lilac, and bee balm. It is unsightly, but not lethal. If mildew is a problem in your area, you can reduce the severity of infestation by dusting plants with garden sulfur or fungicidal soap each year in early summer before the mildew shows (sulfur is nontoxic to people and the environment). Repeat the application following heavy rain.

In early spring when garden phlox reaches 6 to 8 inches tall, select six to eight of the strongest shoots to keep intact. With a sharp knife or pruners, snip off the remaining shoots at ground level. This will expose the shoots that you've left to better air circulation and reduce powdery mildew infestation.

MOSS PHLOX
Phlox subulata

Zones: 2–9

Bloom Time: Early spring

Light: Full sun

Height: 6–9 in.

Interest: Carpets of flowers in many bright colors

Moss phlox's cheerful disposition makes it indispensable in the spring garden. After the drab gray of winter, when any color would be welcome, this creeping evergreen carpets the ground with bright flowers of blue, pink, purple, red, or white. Often found in old cemeteries, moss phlox spreads widely but not rampantly, doesn't mind being mowed during summer, and requires next to no care. All moss phlox selections have the same spreading habit.

HOW TO GROW

Moss phlox requires full sun and any well-drained soil with low fertility (in other words, don't feed it). After flowering, cut the plants back with hedge shears to half their size to encourage compact growth. Propagate by dividing clumps as soon as the flowers fade. Alternatively, try stem cuttings (page 37).

WHERE TO GROW

Use moss phlox as an edging for borders or along paths, or plant it in rock gardens or where it can cascade down a stone wall. It naturalizes well in lawns that are mowed long (no lower than 3 to 4 inches), and it also looks great in a spring window box. Moss phlox is lovely combined with dwarf spring bulbs in large pots or window boxes. After the moss phlox blooms in the window box, transplant it in the garden.

Top Choices

- *P.* 'Blue Hills' has deep blue blossoms with notched petals.

- *P.* 'Candy Stripe' has pink flowers with a striking white stripe on each petal.

- *P.* 'Crimson Beauty' has intense crimson red blossoms and sometimes blooms a second time.

- *P.* 'Emerald Blue' is a vigorous plant with pale blue blossoms and rich, dark green foliage. 'Emerald Pink' is similar with pink blossoms.

- *P.* 'White Delight' has pure white blossoms on large spreading plants.

- *P.* x *lilacina* hybrids include 'Millstream Coral Eye' (white with a coral center) and 'Millstream Daphne' (clear pink).

Garden Companions

Moss phlox's low habit makes it a natural companion to many of the smaller spring bulbs and other carpet-forming spring plants.

- BASKET-OF-GOLD
- DWARF BEARDED IRISES
- DWARF DAFFODILS
- PERENNIAL CANDYTUFT
- ROCK CRESSES
- SNOW-IN-SUMMER
- SPANISH BLUEBELLS
- SPECIES TULIPS

GRASS IN YOUR PHLOX?

Moss phlox is often planted near grassy areas to add spring color to green lawns. While most weeds are quickly smothered beneath the dense, compact growth of moss phlox, grass is another matter. Once grass becomes established amid your phlox, your neat perennial patch can become a weedy mess instead.

To remove the pesky grass, dig up moss phlox plants with a garden fork. Gently clean away any pieces of grass and replant.

OBEDIENT PLANT

Physostegia virginiana

Zones: 2–9

Bloom Time: Late summer

Light: Full sun

Height: 24–36 in.

Interest: Showy flower spikes in shades of pink and white

Obedient plant makes a bright splash of showy spikes of pink, purplish pink, or white blossoms in the late-summer garden. Flowers appear in spiky clusters atop square-stemmed shoots that are clothed with bright green foliage. The variegated form is simply dazzling. The plant gets its name from the fact that if you move individual flowers with your fingers to one side of the stem, they remain in their new location.

HOW TO GROW

Obedient plant will grow in almost any garden soil, but in dry ones it will be shorter and less vigorous. Some varieties spread quickly, making them especially useful in meadow gardens of native or naturalized plants but disobedient nuisances in well-kept borders, especially in the South. Taller varieties require staking or cutting back to half their height in early July. Propagation is easy—dig up, divide, and replant the basal shoots in early spring. Obedient plant is not bothered by pests.

WHERE TO GROW

Obedient plant is perfect for a mixed border, where its color provides a welcome boost when earlier bloomers have lost their charm. Plant some in a cutting garden, too—the spikes hold up well in water and their obedience will impress your friends!

Top Choices

- *P.* 'Summer Snow' has pure white flowers on 36-inch plants with dark green foliage. 'Alba' is similar except that it has invasive tendencies; avoid it in well-manicured borders.

- *P.* 'Variegata' is loved for its striking variegated foliage and flowers of rosy pink on stems 36 inches tall. It's a plant that is so dramatic you'll either love it or hate it!

- *P.* 'Vivid' is a compact grower with intense magenta pink flowers on 24- to 30-inch plants. It is especially good as a cut flower.

PROPAGATING PLANTS BY DIVISION

To increase the number of most plants by division, follow these easy steps:

1 In early spring, as soon as new shoots poke through the ground, dig up the entire crown and shake off excess soil.

2 Using a sharp pair of pruners, cut off individual shoots 4 to 6 inches long with some roots still attached. (Some plants pull apart easily without the need for cutting the stems.) For plants that spread vigorously, don't dig up the entire plant, just loosen the earth around the outer shoots and snip them off for replanting. When planting the shoots, make sure to work the soil well and amend first.

3 Dig a hole large enough so the roots can be spread out before covering them with soil.

BALLOON FLOWER

Platycodon grandiflorus

Zones: 3–8

Bloom Time: Summer

Light: Full sun in the North; part sun in the South

Height: 15–30 in.

Interest: Balloonlike flower buds followed by large, showy flowers over a long season

This tough relative of bellflower is a colorful, well-behaved plant that adds a bright note wherever it is planted. Before the flower buds open, they look like small balloons—hence the common name, balloon flower. The buds open into wide, upward-facing, five-pointed chalices. Balloon flower is free flowering and long-lived, requires little or no maintenance, is useful as a cut flower, and suffers from no pests—what more could you ask of a flowering plant?

HOW TO GROW

Balloon flower grows well in full sun except in the South, where it likes shelter from the afternoon rays. Plant in well-drained, average garden soil. Balloon flower gets a later spring start than many plants, so mark its location well to avoid damaging dormant crowns during early-spring garden work. Taller varieties may need staking; for a more natural look, grow them with baby's-breath, whose foamy stems will intertwine with and hold up those of the balloon flower. To make bushier plants, pinch the growing tips when they reach 12 inches and don't worry about the "bleeding"; it will soon stop.

WHERE TO GROW

Plant balloon flower with impunity in mixed borders, rock gardens, and containers. It blends well with every other color. Shorter varieties are ideal for window boxes or for edging a path. They also make an astonishing ground cover, which from a distance looks like blue pools of water. Plant ballon flower with anything except the most vigorously spreading perennials.

Top Choices

- *P.* 'Albus' is a white-flowered variety with snowy blossoms on 30- to 40- inch stems.

- *P.* 'Double Blue' has two rows of blue petals; the flower stems grow 15 to 24 inches high.

- *P.* 'Sentimental Blue', at a compact 15 inches, is free flowering and perhaps the best selection for containers. It is also the best variety to use for a ground cover.

- *P.* Fuji is a seed mixture from Japan with blue, pink, and white forms on 30-inch spikes. It was developed as a cut flower but is also suitable for planting in borders.

TREATING CUT FLOWERS THAT BLEED

Balloon flowers (also bluestars, butterfly weeds, some bellflowers, and Oriental poppies) bleed when they are cut. To stop the bleeding, singe the end of each stem immediately after cutting with a quick touch from the flame of a match or a lighter. Flaming the stem ends of these plants will extend their vase life; it will not enhance flowers that don't bleed.

IN THE PINK

Though most varieties of balloon flower are blue, there are some charming pink types that add variety and beauty to the garden.

- *P.* 'Shell Pink'
- *P.* 'Seashell'
- *P.* 'Roseus Plenus'

BLACK-EYED SUSAN

Rudbeckia fulgida 'Goldsturm'

Zones: 3–9

Bloom Time: Mid-summer until hard frost

Light: Full sun to light shade

Height: 18–30 in.

Interest: So many black-eyed, golden daisies they all but obscure the foliage

This selection of the black-eyed Susan is considered by some to be one of the world's great garden plants. In late summer, few plants produce as many blossoms. The flowers are 2 to 3 inches across and are a deep golden yellow with an almost black, cone-shaped center. The plant's dazzling color and free-flowering habit make it a favorite with landscapers and gardeners who want to make a colorful impression. Black-eyed Susan is a low-maintenance perennial with a rugged persona inherited from its prairie roots.

HOW TO GROW

Grow black-eyed Susan in any sunny spot in well-drained soil. In the Southeast it is best grown in part shade. Propagate by dividing the crowns in early spring as new shoots appear. Seed propagation is also possible, but the seedlings may differ from their parent. Black-eyed Susan is relatively pest-free and easy-care.

WHERE TO GROW

This is a must grow plant that blends well with a surprisingly wide array of other colors. Use black-eyed Susan in the border, as a ground cover for sunny spots, or plant it in large groups in the flower or vegetable garden for cutting. As a container plant, it is unsurpassed for late-summer color. Enjoy the seed heads in winter as they poke through snow and provide food for seed-eating birds, then cut back the plants in early spring.

Top Choices

- *R. nitida* 'Autumn Sun' makes a great back-of-the-border plant with its 4- to 7-foot height and bright lemon yellow, green-centered flowers.

- *R. laciniata* 'Gold Drop', also known as the cutleaf coneflower, has lemon yellow, double flowers on 3- to 4-foot plants.

- *R. l.* 'Goldquelle' shows true to its name with shining, fully double, bright yellow blossoms on 5- to 6-foot stems.

Garden Companions

Black-eyed Susan is compatible with many other garden plants, seemingly invited to every garden. For a nice contrast in color and visual texture, plant it near any of these plants:

- BEE BALM
- BLUEBEARDS
- BUTTERFLY BUSHES
- FRIKART'S ASTER
- MAIDEN GRASS
- MEXICAN BUSH SAGE
- PURPLE CONEFLOWER
- SEDUM 'AUTUMN JOY'

TESTING DRAINAGE

Black-eyed Susan needs well-drained soil. To test your soil for drainage, dig a 2-foot-deep hole and fill it with water. If the water disappears after 24 hours or less, the soil's drainage is fine for black-eyed Susan. If some water remains, the soil is probably fine for plants that prefer a slightly damp location, such as Joe-Pye weed. If you want to grow black-eyed Susan there, you'll need to mix in several inches of compost and good topsoil to create a raised bed, which will improve drainage.

PURPLE SAGE
Salvia x sylvestris

Zones: 4–10

Bloom Time: Summer

Light: Full sun

Height: 18–36 in.

Interest: Rich, dark bluish violet spikes on compact, well-behaved plants

Purple sage is a free-flowering plant with dark-colored blossoms that contrast pleasantly with most other shades. *S. x sylvestris* is often sold as (and is very similar to) *S. x superba*. Both are choice hybrids that make outstanding garden plants. Both have narrow, dark blue to purple flower spikes on stems that grow from 18 to 36 inches tall, depending on the variety. The foliage is a pleasing gray-green and clothes the well-branched stems. There is a great deal of confusion in catalogs about the correct names for these plants—they hybridize so readily that growers are sometimes not sure what they have.

HOW TO GROW
All sages prefer average, well-drained garden soil and most tolerate drought rather well. The named varieties are best propagated by stem cuttings in early summer,

before they flower. They are easy to grow from collected or purchased seeds, but the offspring won't be identical to the parent.

WHERE TO GROW

Sage is drought-tolerant and performs well both in cool northern climates and in hot ones. In the Deep South, it prefers part shade; tall varieties have a tendency to lose their tidy habit in part shade, though.

Top Choices

- *S.* 'Blue Hill' has rich violet-blue flowers on 18-inch-tall stems.

- *S.* 'Blue Queen' flowers are rich violet-blue on 18- to 24-inch plants.

- *S.* 'East Friesland' features deep purple spikes with maroon bracts. Stems are 18 inches tall.

- *S.* 'May Night' grows to 18 inches with dark purple flowers.

- *S.* 'Rose Queen' has rose-colored blossoms on 24-inch, rose-tinted stems.

- *S.* 'Rose Wine' grows to 18 inches tall with rose-pink flowers.

GROWING STRONG PURPLE SAGE

Purple sage looks best when it has strong, upright flower stalks. Unfortunately, too many gardeners have weak, floppy plants instead. Here are three easy steps to prevent the condition:

1 To grow the strongest plants, be sure to plant purple sage in full sun.

2 Too much fertilizer or organic matter can produce weak stems. Go light on both.

3 Be conservative with water, soaking the soil only after it has had time to dry out from the previous watering .

PROPAGATING HYBRIDS

Many hybrids are best propagated by division (see page 103). The best time to divide plants differs a little with each plant, but the best time to divide many perennials is early spring. Plants divided at this time of year generally do best because the roots are rich with carbohydrates from the previous growing season.

PINCUSHION FLOWER
Scabiosa caucasica

Zones: 3–8

Bloom Time: All summer to frost

Light: Full sun

Height: 18–24 in.

Interest: Compact plant that blooms its head off with lavender blue, white, or lilac-pink flowers

Pincushion flower's prolific blooming habit has made it one of the most popular perennials around. Its lovely lavender-blue, white, or lilac-pink, 2-inch blossoms first appear in early summer and continue until hard frost—in mild climates it continues to bloom during winter. Of course, butterflies love it too!

HOW TO GROW

Pincushion flower requires sun and well-drained soil that is slightly acidic to slightly alkaline. Provide extra water during dry spells. To encourage more abundant blooming, remove dead flower heads regularly—it's a small chore for a plant that gives so much in return. Propagation is by division, but who would want to give up so many blossoms for a single season when purchased plants are relatively inexpensive?

WHERE TO GROW

This unsurpassed bloomer is ideal for containers or for the front of a border. It also looks stunning planted in a bed with small ornamental grasses. Its ability to flower during the shorter days of winter makes it an ideal pot plant for a cool conservatory or greenhouse—with an occasional excursion indoors for special events. Because pincushion flower blooms so long, locate it with other plants that span the growing season from spring to fall, including daylilies, Carpathian bellflowers, mallow, purple sages, hollyhocks, and Stokes' asters.

Top Choices

- S. 'Blue Perfection' is a heavy bloomer with lavender-blue flowers.

- S. 'Fama' is an elegant plant with large lilac-blue flowers over 3 inches in diameter on 24-inch stems.

- S. 'Compliment' bears large blue flowers accented with dark lilac on 24-inch-tall stems from spring to summer.

- S. 'Perfecta Alba' has pure white, shaggy flowers on 18-inch stems.

- S. columbaria 'Butterfly Blue' has abundant blue flowers that begin to appear in summer and continue to fall. It is one of the heaviest bloomers of all and grows only 15 inches tall.

- S. c. 'Pink Mist' is more lilac-pink than true pink. The flowers, which appear from spring to fall, are beautiful and plentiful.

BUTTERFLIES IN THE GARDEN

Butterflies add a breath of life and movement to any garden. To create a butterfly garden:

- Provide an area that is open to the sun and protected from heavy winds.

- When selecting plants for the butterfly garden, remember that pincushion flowers, daylilies, bellflowers, and butterfly weeds are especially attractive to nectar-seeking butterflies.

- Add a simple birdbath to furnish butterflies with water.

- Avoid using pesticides, as many of these kill butterflies and their larvae (caterpillars) along with pests.

SELECTING HAND PRUNERS

The best pruning shears to use in the garden are bypass pruners. This type operates like scissors and has two cutting blades that slip past each other as they slice. The cuts are very clean with little crushing of plant tissue.

Bypass pruners often have handles ergonomically designed to ease hand fatigue, a cushion stop to relieve shock, a sap groove to channel away plant sap, and a wire-cutting notch.

SEDUM

Sedum 'Autumn Joy'

Zones: 3–9

Bloom Time: Late summer to fall

Light: Full to part sun

Height: 18–24 in.

Interest: Abundant flowers that vary in shades of pink and red as the season passes; much loved by butterflies and bees; attractive, succulent foliage

A showy sedum cultivar, 'Autumn Joy' is one of the most popular flowering perennials of late summer. It has such a strong personality that it dominates its surroundings. Green buds appear in late summer and look like broccoli heads (but don't eat them). Gradually they turn light pink, mature to a warm pink, then become rusty red, and finally a rich brown. The flowers are long-lasting and dry well for winter arrangements. The fleshy foliage is an attractive grayish green and very succulent. In winter, lightly dusted with snow, 'Autumn Joy' adds a strong architectural feature to the garden.

HOW TO GROW

'Autumn Joy' grows in almost any soil, and is completely maintenance-free, pest-free, and absolutely reliable—in other words, you can't miss with this garden favorite.

The rusty brown seed heads are one of the joys of winter gardens. Plants often self-sow. Watch for the small plants to appear in the garden and transplant to a new location. Large clumps should be divided every three to four years so they don't become weak and floppy.

WHERE TO GROW

It is probably impossible (and maybe illegal) to have a garden without at least one clump of 'Autumn Joy'. Many gardeners can't resist planting lots of it—in perennial and mixed borders, by itself in huge drifts, or in containers. Plant enough to use for flower arrangements. It is a spectacular addition.

Other Sedums

- *S.* 'Brilliant', 'Meteor', and 'Stardust' feature raspberry red, rose, and white flowers, respectively, on 24-inch plants.

- *S.* 'Matrona', a recent introduction, has attractive dark foliage and dark pinkish red flowers on 24- to 30-inch plants.

- *S.* 'Ruby Glow' is another dwarf plant reaching 6 to 8 inches tall, with rosy crimson flowers set off with fleshy gray-blue leaves.

- *S. spurium* 'John Creech' is a charming ground cover growing just 2 inches tall with a mantle of pink flowers in late spring to early summer.

Garden Companions

Sedum 'Autumn Joy' is a cornerstone of the late-summer and early-fall garden. It looks best nestled among other late-flowering perennials such as:

- BLACK-EYED SUSAN
- GLOBE THISTLE
- NEW ENGLAND ASTER
- RUSSIAN SAGE
- WHITE CONEFLOWER
- WHITE OBEDIENT FLOWER

STOCKING A
ROCK GARDEN

Most rock gardens are stocked with low-growing, hardy plants that tolerate sun and difficult conditions. They require little maintenance and can form a visually stunning garden, even in a small area.

Because rock gardens tend to be small, the most popular rock-garden plants are slow-growers, assuring that the garden can be enjoyed for years before the plants grow too large. Some of the best rock garden plants include 'Ruby Glow' sedum, basket-of-gold, speedwell, 'Munstead Dwarf' lavender, moss phlox, and Carpathian bellflower.

LAMB'S-EARS
Stachys byzantina

Zones: 5–9

Bloom Time: Early summer

Light: Full to part sun

Height: 6–8 in. (foliage); 12–15 in. (flowers)

Interest: Large, velvety, silver-gray leaves

The soft, furry, silvery gray leaves of lamb's-ears are irresistible to children and sensualists. Its 12- to 15-inch flower spikes are not showy (the small lavender-pink blooms are almost hidden by the silver-gray stem leaves) and are thought to distract from the more appealing foliage. For this reason, many gardeners remove them as soon as they appear. Plants are spreading, but not invasively so, and gradually form clumps measuring 3 to 4 feet across.

HOW TO GROW

Lamb's-ears requires well-drained garden soil, so avoid overhead watering, especially in hot, humid weather. Buried soaker hoses work best. In the Southeast, heat and humidity and frequent thunderstorms keep the foliage wet. As a result, the plants "melt out" in summer, but bounce back in fall. During the winter they remain fresh and evergreen, which makes them worth a place in the garden despite their summer sulk.

WHERE TO GROW

Lamb's-ears is usually planted at the edges of borders or in spots where it can spill over paths and terraces—the better to have its leaves petted by all who pass. While not a star in its own right, it acts as the perfect background for colorful companions; any moderate-sized plant makes a good neighbor. Lamb's-ears can be used as a ground cover under roses or among dwarf conifers where it is content to play a supporting role.

Top Choices

- S. 'Big Ears' has large leaves, as the name implies, and is the best choice for hot, humid weather.

- S. 'Helene von Stein' is another non-flowering form with big, silvery leaves and few or no flowers.

- S. 'Silver Carpet' may be your choice if you prefer a plant that doesn't produce flower spikes.

REMOVING
FLOWER HEADS

Since the flower stems of lamb's-ears detract from the beauty of the plant, flowering shoots should be snipped off as soon as they are identifiable—when stems show above the foliage bearing much smaller leaves than the large, furry basal leaves. Snip the stems as close to the crown as possible.

CONTROLLING
LEAF ROT

Lamb's-ears is hardy and easy to grow, but in very wet or humid weather it can acquire leaf spot. The foliage develops tan to brown spots that can enlarge, turning the leaves a mushy brown.

To control this disease, avoid getting the leaves wet as much as possible. If spots appear, remove damaged leaves promptly and discard. Once conditions dry out, lamb's-ears bounce back quickly, producing a new crop of disease-free, soft and fuzzy leaves.

STOKES' ASTER

Stokesia laevis

Zones: 5–9

Bloom Time: Summer

Light: Full to part sun

Height: 18–24 in.

Interest: Very large, soft, wisteria blue flowers, like giant cornflowers, over a long season

The large (4-inch-diameter) flowers of Stokes' aster appear in early summer and last until late summer in the North; the plant blooms all winter in Florida and almost all year in Mediterranean climates such as southern California. Stokes' aster has smooth, bright green, spear-shaped leaves that are evergreen in mild climates. The plants are compact growers, never outgrowing the space in which they are planted. Stokes' aster makes a superb cut flower.

HOW TO GROW

This southeastern native thrives everywhere in average, well-drained soil. Soggy soil in winter results in certain death. In the South, Stokes' aster prefers a little shade from the afternoon sun. Remove spent blossoms to encourage more flowers. Propagate by division in very early spring. New plants can also be started from seeds, but named selections only come true from division.

WHERE TO GROW

To fully enjoy the large but delicate flowers, plant Stokes' aster close to the front of the border. It's also suitable for rock gardens and containers—even window boxes in cool climates.

Top Choices

- *S.* 'Blue Danube' is a deep blue selection that blooms relatively early in the year.

- *S.* 'Klaus Jelito' has large (to 4 inches across), wisteria blue blossoms.

- *S.* 'Lutea' and 'Mary Gregory' are the oddballs with pale yellow flowers.

- *S.* 'Omega Skyrocket' is exceptional in that it grows over 4 feet tall with light blue flowers.

- *S.* 'Purple Parasols' is a new variety that opens blue but soon deepens to deep violet-purple.

- *S.* 'Silver Moon' and 'Alba' are both pure white and are equally as vigorous as the blue varieties.

Garden Companions

The subtle hues and long bloom time of Stokes' aster make it a fine neighbor to a varied host of plants in the perennial border, including:

- BLUE FESCUE
- CALAMINT
- COLUMBINES
- DWARF GOATSBEARD
- LADY'S-MANTLES
- LAMB'S-EARS
- SPEEDWELLS
- THREADLEAF COREOPSIS
- YARROWS

WATERING JUST ENOUGH

Many perennials grow best when they receive about 1 inch of water per week during the growing season. This is easy to recommend, but it can be very frustrating to try to figure out just how much water is one inch. Here's an easy way.

Before watering, set an empty tuna fish can into the garden so the rim is flush with the soil.

When you turn on the sprinkler, time how long it takes for the can to fill up with water. That's about how long you need to water to put an inch of water on the garden.

SPEEDWELL
Veronica

Zones: 3–10

Bloom Time: All summer until frost

Light: Full to part sun

Height: 12–24 in.

Interest: Masses of blue, pink, or white flower spikes

Speedwell, more commonly known by its botanical name, *Veronica*, has been around for years but recently has become very popular among perennial growers for its showy flower spikes and its prodigious blooming habit. It is remarkably tough in both the cold winters of the North and the heat and humidity of the Southeast. Veronica is an easy grower and is virtually trouble-free. The blooms last well in water if cut when half the flowers on a spike are open.

HOW TO GROW
Veronica prefers average, well-drained garden soil and will tolerate dry conditions. It thrives in southern heat, but also flourishes in the cool North. If grown in part shade, it may flop over, so support the plant with short

lengths of brushwood. Otherwise the only care required is deadheading.

WHERE TO GROW

Plant veronica at the edges of perennial borders, spilling over paths and stone walls, and in rock gardens, window boxes, and containers. Don't forget to plant some to cut for baskets of blossoms all summer long.

Top Choices

- V. 'Barcarolle', 'Minuet', and 'Red Fox' are all pink-flowered selections on plants that grow 12 to 18 inches tall.

- V. 'Blue Peter' produces long, deep blue flower spikes on 30- to 36-inch plants.

- V. 'Crater Lake Blue' blooms in a deep gentian blue on spreading 12- to 18-inch plants.

- V. 'Goodness Grows' is as close to an ever-blooming veronica as there is. From spring to fall it bears spikes of deep blue flowers on 14-inch stems.

- V. prostrata 'Heavenly Blue', as the name implies, blooms in a brilliant sapphire blue on 6- to 8-inch stems.

- V. 'Sunny Border Blue' grows 18 to 24 inches tall with violet-blue spikes and slightly crinkled foliage.

Garden Companions

Veronica is one of the best supporting actors in the garden, surrounding other plants with color and interesting form. Consider planting it with:

- CAMPIONS
- PERENNIAL GERANIUMS
- JAPANESE BLOOD GRASS
- 'BATH'S PINK' GARDEN PINK
- SEA HOLLY
- SHASTA DAISIES
- SUNDROPS
- SIBERIAN IRISES
- THREADLEAF COREOPSIS

EDGING PLANTS

Edging plants are low-growers that are most often used at a border's edge or along a garden path. They are often used along walkways, softening edges as they spill out over the path. To avoid monotony, it's best to plant several different plants to act as edgers; plants of all one kind give the garden a rigid, linear, formal look that is not complementary to the habit of most perennials.

GLOSSARY

Accent plant: A plant that draws attention by its extraordinary display.

Acidic soil: Soil with a pH value of less than 7.0.

Alkaline soil: Soil with a pH value of more than 7.0.

Biennial: A plant that grows vegetatively one year, produces flowers, fruits, and seeds the next, and then dies.

Border: A garden bed that is designed to edge or frame something, often backed by a wall, hedge, or fence.

Bract: A colorful leaflike structure that appears below a flower, such as the showy part of a dogwood or poinsettia "flower."

Brushwood: Twigs cut in late winter to use for staking plants.

Clump: A group of stems or underground shoots with several vegetative buds.

Cottage gardening: Gardens based on an English style of gardening in which many plants are placed in a dense and seemingly random fashion.

Cross-pollinate: When a flower of one plant is fertilized by the pollen from a flower of another plant.

Crown: The part of a plant where the roots are attached to the shoots.

Cultivation: To work the soil by digging, forking, hoeing, or using a mechanical device.

Cutting garden: A bed for growing flowers to harvest.

Deadheading: The removal of spent flowers to tidy up a plant and force it to put its energy into producing more flowers instead of seeds.

Division: A method of propagation in which the crown of a plant is separated into two or more pieces.

Double-flowered: A flower that has more the usual number of petals.

Flaming: A technique that burns the cut end of a stem to stop it from "bleeding" sap (see page 105).

Flush: Abundant new growth produced after dormancy or being cut back.

Foundation plant: A plant placed next to a building to hide the foundation or soften the hard architectural lines.

Genus: A group of closely related species.

Ground cover: Plants that are used to cover bare ground; they usually spread to form dense colonies that choke out weeds.

Humus: Dark, fine-textured material that results from organic material reaching an advanced stage of decay.

Hybrid: A plant resulting from the cross-pollination of genetically dissimilar plants.

Inflorescence: The flowering part of a plant.

Interplant: To place plants between other plants to extend seasonal interest—such as spring bulbs among plants that develop later, such as hostas.

Island bed: A flower bed that you can walk around.

Leaf compost: Organic matter made from leaves that have been allowed to decay. Also called leaf mold.

Limestone: A soil amendment containing calcium; it slowly raises the pH of a soil so it is more alkaline (basic). Dolomitic limestone is the safest form to use. If soil tests indicate adequate magnesium, then calcitic limestone is the safest form to use.

Meadow gardening: Growing plants in an open area resembling an uncultivated field. Undesirable species are cut back or eliminated.

Mixed border: A border containing a combination of different types of plants such as annuals, bulbs, perennials, and shrubs.

Mulch: A layer of organic or inorganic material placed around plants to hold in moisture and reduce weeds.

Organic matter: Decayed animal and plant remains, such as compost, leaf mold, or aged manure, used as a soil conditioner. See also humus.

Peat moss: A usually weed-free form of organic matter created by the partial decomposition of sphagnum moss. It increases soil acidity.

Pinching: Snipping out (or using fingernails to literally pinch out) the growing point of a plant to promote fuller, bushier plants.

Powdery mildew: A disease that coats the upper surfaces of leaves and flowers with an unsightly pale gray or white, dustlike growth.

Propagate: To create new plants.

Raised bed: A bed that is higher than the surrounding area, often contained within a low retaining wall composed of rocks, bricks, logs, or boards.

Recurrent bloom (repeat blooming): Blooming after the main flush of flowers has passed.

Rhizome: A horizontal stem at or under the soil surface, such as the root of a bearded iris.

Semidouble: A flower with two or three rows of petals.

Semiwoody: A perennial that has shrublike stems.

Single-flowered: A flower with the standard number of petals, often a single row.

Species: A group of plants within a genus that are more or less identical.

Spike: A long, usually unbranched flower stem.

Spur: A projection from a flower or sepal that is either tubelike or saclike. Most columbine flowers are spurred.

Stamen: A flower's male reproductive organ, where pollen is produced.

Stem cuttings: Pieces of shoots cut from a plant to create new plants.

True to variety: A plant whose seedling offspring are identical in appearance to the parent plant.

Tuber: A thick, food-storing, underground stem—for example, the root of a daylily.

Underplant: To plant flowers or bulbs beneath the canopy of a larger plant to add color to the garden without taking up additional space.

Variegated leaves: Leaves that are patterned in a different color.

Variety: A subdivision of a species, commonly used in place of the horticultural term *cultivar*, which is a cultivated variety.

Well-drained soil: Soil that drains relatively quickly, even after heavy rain.

Wet feet: A term for a plant that is sitting in waterlogged soil.

Zone Map

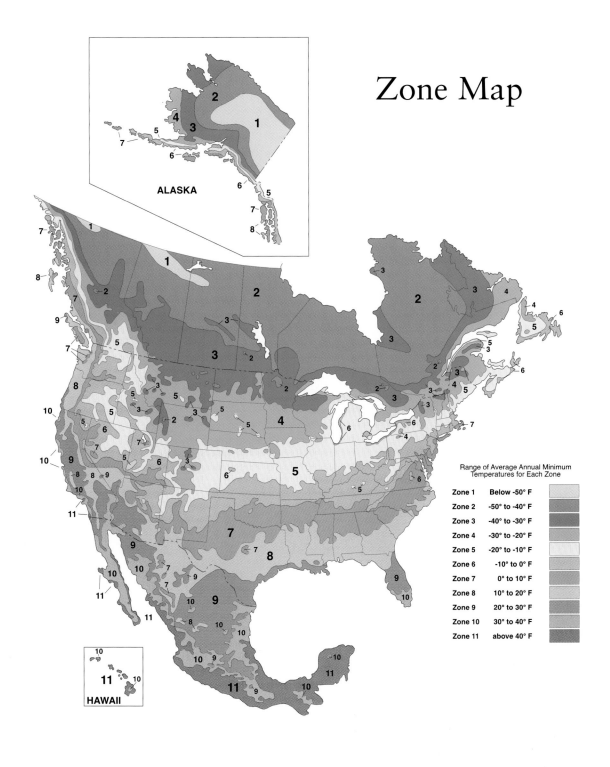

ALASKA

HAWAII

Range of Average Minimum
Temperatures for Each Zone

Zone 1	Below -50° F
Zone 2	-50° to -40° F
Zone 3	-40° to -30° F
Zone 4	-30° to -20° F
Zone 5	-20° to -10° F
Zone 6	-10° to 0° F
Zone 7	0° to 10° F
Zone 8	10° to 20° F
Zone 9	20° to 30° F
Zone 10	30° to 40° F
Zone 11	above 40° F

INDEX

PHOTOGRAPHY & ILLUSTRATION CREDITS

David Cavagnaro
Front cover, title page, 12, 17, 36, 48, 54, 56, 59, 60, 66, 68, 70, 82, 88, 100, 102, 116

Anna Dewdney, illustrator
11, 23, 29, 35, 39, 45, 49, 55, 61, 71, 75, 91, 99, 105, 115

Thomas E. Eltzroth
64

Derek Fell
10, 32, 84, 80, 86, 96, 98, 104, 110

H. Armstrong Roberts, Inc.
16

Bill Johnson
114

Jerry Pavia, Jerry Pavia Photography, Inc.
20, 28, 30, 50, 52, 69, 72, 76, 84, 92, 108, 118

Richard Shiell
67, 73, 78

Steven M. Still
22, 62

Joseph G. Strauch Jr.
14, 18, 24, 26, 34, 38, 44, 46, 58, 90, 106, 112

White Flower Farm, Inc.
40, 42, 94

Storey Communications, Inc.
Pownal, Vermont

President: M. John Storey
Executive Vice President: Martha M. Storey
Chief Operating Officer: Dan Reynolds
Director of Custom Publishing: Deirdre Lynch
Project Manager: Barbara Weiland
Author: Michael H. Dodge
Book Design: Betty Kodela
Design Assistance: Jen Rork
Horticultural Edit: Charles W. G. Smith; Liz Stell